HANDBOOK

of

REVOLUTIONARY

WARFARE

A Guide to the Armed Phase of the African Revolution

To The African Guerrilla

AUTHOR'S NOTE

This book has been written during my stay in Conakry. Previous notes I made for a manual of guerrilla warfare for African freedom fighters were left behind in Ghana when I departed for Hanoi on 21st February 1966. The manuscript was handed over to imperialist and neo- colonialist intelligence organisations by the military and police traitors.

This HANDBOOK, presenting a completely new approach will, I hope, help to make possible the successful completion of the armed phase of the African revolutionary struggle for total emancipation and an All-African Union Govern- ment.

The Black Power movement in the U.S.A., and the struggles of peoples of African descent in the Caribbean, South America and elsewhere, form an integral part of the African politico-military revolutionary struggle. Our victory will be their victory also, and the victory of all the revolu- tionary, oppressed and exploited masses of the world who are challenging the capitalist, imperialist and neo-colonialist power structure of reaction and counter-revolution.

Conakry, Guinea.
30th July 1968.

RULES OF DISCIPLINE

1. Obey orders in all your actions.

2. Do not take a single needle or piece of thread from the masses.

3. Turn in everything captured.

4. Speak politely.

5. Pay fairly for what you buy.

6. Return everything you borrow.

7. Pay for anything you damage.

8. Do not hit or swear at people.

9. Do not damage crops.

10. Do not take liberties with women.

11. Do not ill-treat captives.

12. Keep your eyes and ears open.

13. Know the enemy within.

14. Always guide and protect the children.
15. Always be the servant of the people.

The guerrilla is the masses in arms

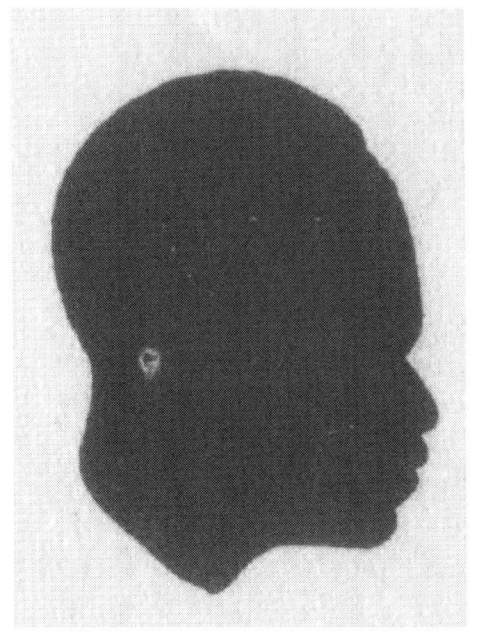

BOOK ONE

KNOW THE ENEMY

PREFACE

The new phase of the armed revolutionary struggle in Africa embraces the entire continent. It is essential that we know what we fight, and why we fight. Imperialism and neo- colonialism must be broken down into their component parts so that we can clearly see them. We must know their world strategy.

In this book I have attempted to show the nature and extent of imperialist and neo-colonialist aggression, and our objectives in the struggle for the freedom and the political unification of Africa.

CHAPTER ONE

THE WORLD STRATEGY OF IMPERIALISM

Know the enemy

A number of external factors affect the African situation, and if our liberation struggle is to be placed in correct per- spective and we are to KNOW THE ENEMY, the impact of these factors must be fully grasped. First among them is imperialism, for it is mainly against exploitation and poverty that our peoples revolt. It is therefore of paramount importance to set out the strategy of imperialism in clear terms :

The means used by the enemy to ensure the continued economic exploitation of our territories.

The nature of the attempts made to destroy the liberation movement.

- Once the components of the enemy's strategy are deter- mined, we will be in a position to outline the correct strategy for our own struggle in terms of our actual situation and in accordance with our objectives.

Before the Second World War, the world (excluding the USSR, China, etc.) was divided into :

Capitalist states practising orthodox imperialism under the generally known form of imperialism.

Colonial territories which fed the economies of the capitalist imperialist states. (The Latin American territories had already passed from the status of "Spanish" and "Portuguese" colonies to that of neo-colonies.)

However, after the Second World War, serious economic, social and political tensions arose in both spheres.

Inside the capitalist-imperialist states, workers' organisations had become comparatively strong and experienced, and the claims of the working class for a more substantial share of the wealth produced by the capitalist economy could no longer be ignored. The necessity to concede had become all the more imperative since the European capitalist system had been seriously shaken up by the near-holocaust which marked the experience of imperialist wars.

While the capitalist system of exploitation was coming to grips with its internal crises, the world's colonised areas were astir with the upsurge of strong liberation movements. Here again, demands could no longer be cast aside or ignored especially when they were chan- nelled through irresistible mass movements, like the Rassemblement Democratique Africain (RDA), the Parti Démocratique de Guineé (PDG) and the Convention Peoples' Party (CPP) in Ghana. In certain areas, for example in Vietnam,

Kenya and Algeria, direct confrontation demonstrated the readiness of the oppressed peoples to implement their claims with blood and fire.

Both in the colonial territories and in the metropolitan states, the struggle was being waged against the same enemy : international finance capital under its external and internal forms of exploitation, imperialism and capitalism.

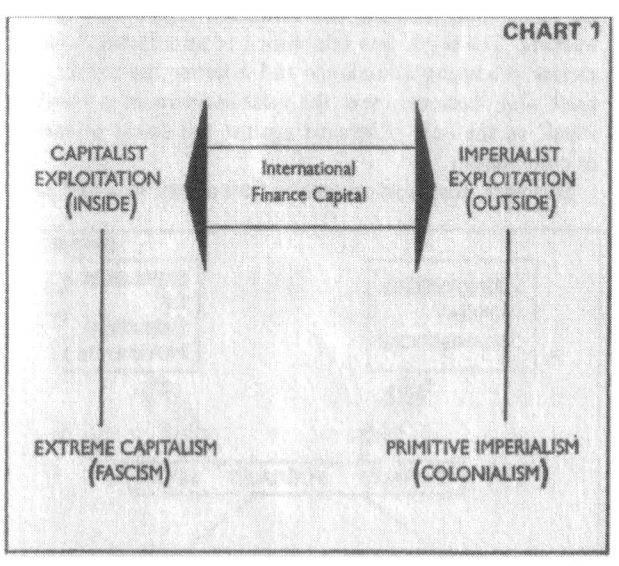

Threatened with disintegration by the double-fisted attack of the working class movement and the liberation movement, capitalism had to launch a series of reforms in order to build a protective armour around the inner workings of its system.

To avoid an internal breakdown of the system under the pressure of the workers' protest movement, the governments of capitalist countries granted their workers certain concessions which did not endanger the basic nature of the capitalist system of exploitation. They gave them social security, higher wages, better working conditions, profess- ional training facilities, and other improvements.

These reforms helped to blur fundamental contradictions, and to remove some of the more glaring injustices while at the same time ensuring the continued exploitation of the workers. The myth was established of an affluent capitalist society promising abundance and a better life for all. The basic aim, however, was the establishment of a "welfare state" as the only safeguard against the threat of fascism or communism.

However, the problem was to find a way to avoid sacrificing the all-important principle of ever-increasing profits for the owning minority, and also to find the money needed to finance the welfare state.

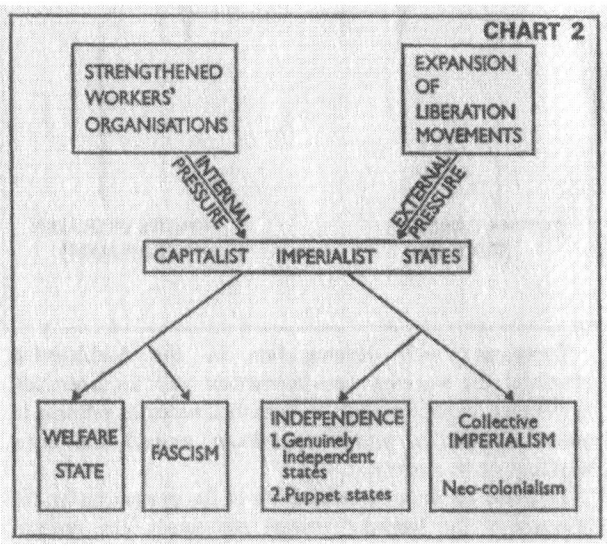

By way of a solution, capitalism proceeded to introduce not only internal reforms, but external reforms designed to raise the extra money needed for the establishment and the maintenance of the welfare state at home. In other words, modern capitalism had come to depend more heavily than before on the exploitation of the material and human re- sources of the colonial territories. On the external front, therefore, it became necessary for international finance capital to carry out reforms in order to eliminate the deadly threat to its supremacy of the liberation movement.

The urgent need for such reforms was made clear by the powerful growth and expansion of the liberation forces in Africa, Asia and Latin America, where revolutionary move- ments had not only seized power but were actually con- solidating their gains. Developments in the USSR, China, Cuba, North Vietnam, North Korea, and in Egypt, Ghana, Guinea, Mali, Algeria and other parts of Africa, showed that not only was the world balance of forces shifting, but that the capitalist-imperialist states were con- fronted with a real danger of encirclement.

Collective imperialism

The modifications introduced by imperialism in its strategy were expressed :

a) through the disappearance of the numerous old- fashioned "colonies" owing exclusive allegiance to a single metropolitan country.

b) through the replacement of "national" imperialisms by a "collective" imperialism in which the USA occupies a leading position.

The roots of this process may be traced back to the period of the Second World War, when the socialist camp was still too small and weak to give decisive assistance to the European working class movement. The workers were therefore all the more easily deflected from the objectives of their struggle, and allowed themselves to be dragged into a bloody war of imperialism.

The Second World War seriously strained the political and economic strength of Europe, although capitalism as a system emerged relatively intact. However, the true winner of the whole contest turned out to be the United States of America. Having helped the allies to win the war, the USA was from then on able to retain its pre-eminent position, and to acquire increasing influence in the economic life of the exhausted European states.

This "internationalisation" or "syndicalisation" enabled US imperialism to forestall temporarily an incipient crisis by fulfilling two *sin qua non* conditions :

I. The need to expand

The US-European post-war alliance not only enabled the USA to benefit from the advantages of the European market, which had hitherto been largely closed to its penetration; but also opened up new horizons in Asia, Africa, and Latin America where the USA had already superceded European supremacy and established neo-colonialist domination.

2. The need to militarise

The militarisation of the US economy, based on the political pretext of the threatening rise of the USSR and later of the People's Republic of China as socialist powers, enabled the USA to postpone its internal crises, first during the "hot" war (1939-1945) and then during the "cold" war (since 1945).

Militarisation served two main purposes:

1. It absorbed, and continues to absorb, an excess of unorganised energy into the intense armaments drive which supports imperialist aggression and many blocs and alliances formed by imperialist powers over the last twenty years.

2. It made possible an expensive policy of paternalist corruption of the poor and oppressed people of the world.

The principle of mutual inter-imperialist assistance whereby American, British, French and West German monopoly capital extends joint control over the wealth of the non-liberated zones of Africa, Latin America and Asia, finds concrete expression in the formation of interlocked international financial institutions and bodies of credit:

International Monetary Fund (IMF), USA 25% of the votes.

International Bank for Reconstruction and Development (IBRD), USA 34% of the votes.

International Development Association (IDA), USA 41% of the votes.

On a lesser scale, Europe as a whole, and West Germany in particular, find profitable outlets for big business in Africa through the agencies of such organisations as the European Common Market (EEC).

The imperialists even make use of the United Nations Organisation in order to camouflage their neo-colonialist objectives. This can be seen, for example in US policy in South Korea and the Congo.

Sham independence

But as far as the imperialists are concerned the real solution to the problem of continued exploitation through con- cessions and reform lies in the concept of "sham-independence". A state can be said to be a neo-colonialist or client state if it is independent de jure and dependent de facto. It is a state where political power lies in the conservative forces of the former colony and where economic power re- mains under the control of international finance capital.

In other words, the country continues to be economically exploited by interests which are alien to the majority of the ex-colonised population but are intrinsic to the world capitalist sector. Such a state is in the grip of neo- colonialism. It has become a client state.

Neo-colonialism

The pre-requisite of a correct and global strategy to defeat neo-colonialism is the ability to discover and expose the way in which a state becomes neo-colonialist. For although a neo-colonialist state enjoys only sham independence it is to all outward appearances independent, and therefore the very roots of neo-colonialism must be traced back to the struggle for independence in a colonial territory.

If the liberation movement is firmly established, the colonial power invariably resorts to a "containment" policy in order to stop any further progress, and to deaden its impact. To achieve this objective, the colonial power uses its arsenal of alliances, its network of military bases, eco- nomic devices such as corruption, sabotage and blackmail, and equally insidious, the psychological weapon of propaganda with a view to impressing on the masses a number of imperialist dogmas :

1. That western democracy and the parliamentary system are the only valid ways of governing; that they constitute the only worth-while model for the indigenous élite by the colonial power.

2. That capitalism, free enterprise, free competition, etc., are the only economic systems capable of

promoting development; that the western powers have mastered the liberal-capitalist technique perfectly; that the colonial territory should become an economic satellite in its own interest; that there is no reason to put an end to the policy of "co-operation" pursued during the colonial regime; and that any attempt to break away would be dangerous, since the colonial power is always ready to give "aid".

3. That the slightest "lapse" on the part of the leaders of the liberation movement could push the country into the grip of "communism" and of "totalitarian dictatorship".

4. That the carve-up agreed upon by the imperialists during the colonial period is fair and sacred; that it would be unthinkable even to attempt to liberate areas in terms of their common cultural and historical links; that the only acceptable version of "liberation" must apply to the artificial units designed by the imperia- lists, and hurriedly labelled "nations" in spite of the fact that they are

neither culturally unified, nor economically self-sufficient.

As a further justification of its policy, imperialism usually resorts to all types of propaganda in order to highlight and exploit differences of religion, culture, race, outlook, and of political ideology among the oppressed masses, or between regions which share a long history of mutual commercial and cultural exchange.

- Such methods aim to orientate the leaders of the libera- tion movements towards a brand of nationalism based on petty-minded and aggressive chauvinism, as well as to steer the liberation movement along a reformist path. The prob- lem of "liberation" is therefore usually raised in terms of a participation of "good" indigenous elements in the administration of the colonised territory, for instance through a policy of "africanisation" devoid of any funda- mental changes in the political, economic and administrative structure of the territory.

The transition to neo-colonialism is marked by a succes- sion of more or less important measures which culminate into a ritual of so-called free elections, mostly organised through methods of intimidation. Local agents, selected by the colonial power as "worthy representatives" are then presented to the people as the champions of national independence, and are immediately given all the superficial attributes of power : a puppet government has been formed.

By the very nature of its essential objective, which is exploitation, neo-colonialism can only flourish in a client state.

When the farce of sham elections to form a puppet gov- ernment proves too difficult to enact, the colonial power tries to divide the liberation movement into a "moderate" wing with which it seeks accommodation, and a militant wing which it endeavours to isolate and to suppress by force.

- In the last resort, neo-colonialists can even set up a bogus "progressive" party or organisation using local agents and maintain an artificial liberation movement which serves both as a worthy partner for negotiations and as an intelligence and/or repression agency against the genuine liberation movement supported by the oppressed masses. Such is the role played by FLING in regard to Guinea-Bissao, and UPA in regard to Angola. And so once more the stage is set for negotiations, autonomy and the formation of a puppet government.

However the machinations of the colonial power will fail wherever the leaders of the struggle for independence main- tain a clear spirit of vigilance, and cultivate genuinely revolutionary qualities.

Then, and only then, does a truly independent government emerge, dedicated to national reconstruction in the liberated territory, and determined to assist all those engaged in anti-imperialist struggle.

Such a government is an obstacle barring the advance of neo-colonialism, and such obstacles must be increased be- cause the example of genuine independence is contagious and will help to fortify extensive zones against imperialist aggression.

Faced with genuine independence, imperialism is increasingly compelled to resort to encirclement and subversion in order to overthrow these popular governments, using such weapons as *coups d'etat,* assassination, mutiny within the party, tribal revolt, palace revolutions, and so on, while at the same time strengthening neighbouring puppet regimes to form a political safety belt, a *cordon sanitaire.*

Therefore, the main sphere in which we must strive to defeat neo-colonialist intrigues is within the movement for true independence; that is, within the progressive political party which forms the government. This is particularly true in the one party state which can only function successfully under socialism. Usually, this ruling party is made up of several groups each with its distinct economic and politi- cal interests. The relative importance of each group in the party and state machinery will determine the course of de- velopment. Imperialist strategy is therefore directed towards bringing into a position of pre-eminence that group which most nearly shares its economic and political views.

If a member of a group which is absolutely opposed to imperialism is in control of the state and party, attempts are made to organise :

Either

1. Assassination or a coup d'état or "palace revolution" which will permit political power to fall into the lap of the rival but pro-imperialist group.

Or

2. A decentralisation of political power within the ruling party, one group being strong in the state machinery, the other strong in the party machine. Even in the state machine, the vital organs are artfully put into the hands of forces ready to parley with imperialists. The nursing of discontent and confusion within the party and among the people, through the spread of conflicting ideologies, rumours of economic run- down, maladministration and

corruption, will per- mit the creation of an atmosphere of dissatisfaction favourable to a change in the personnel of govern- ment. Ostensibly the same party is in power. In truth, a qualitative change in the nature of political power has taken place.

Since the conglomerate nature of the ruling party is the basic fact on which neo-colonialist strategy depends, the main remedial measures must be directed to this sphere, and this problem must be borne in mind even before the achievement of independence. It is essential that positive action should in its dialectical evolution anticipate the seminal disintegration and discover a way of containing the future schismatic tendencies.

Neo-colonialism constitutes the necessary condition for the establishment of welfare states by the imperialist nations. **Just as the welfare state is the internal condition, neo-colonialism is the external condition, for the continued hegemony of international finance capital.**

It is precisely the increasing dependence of the imperialist system on neo-colonialist exploitation on an international scale which renders its existence so precarious, and its future so uncertain.

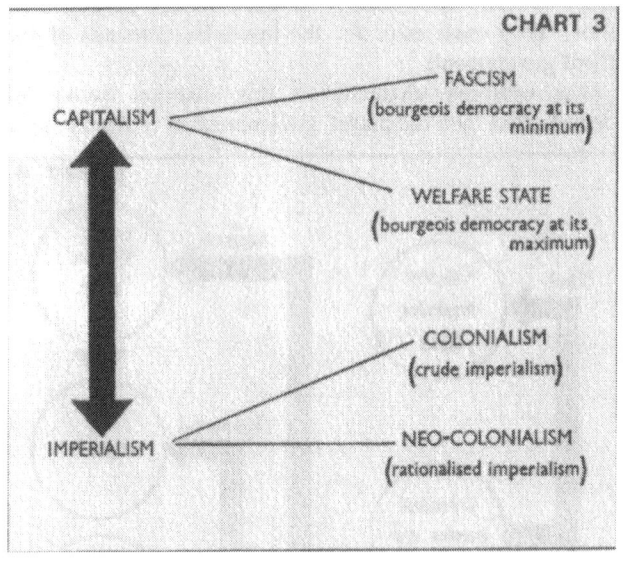

Significantly, the neo-colonialist system costs the capi- talist powers comparatively little, while enormous and in- creasing profits are made. This is shown by the ever-rising graphs representing the turn-over figures of the big capitalist business concerns implanted in the neo-colonialist areas of the world, and by the ever-widening gap between the wealthy and the poor peoples of the world.

In the final analysis, the neo-colonialist system of exploi- tation, which is the external condition for the maintenance of the capitalist welfare state, remains essentially dependent on the production of the neo-colonised workers, who must not only continue to produce under stagnant and continu- ally worsening living conditions, but must produce sub- stantially more than they did in the colonial days. They must do more than satisfy the needs of the metropolitan state. They must cater for the insatiable demands of the client government.

The explosive character of this situation cannot be denied. The neo-colonialist government is virtually in a state of permanent conflict with its own masses, whilst the gap between the puppet administration and neo-colonised workers widens every day.

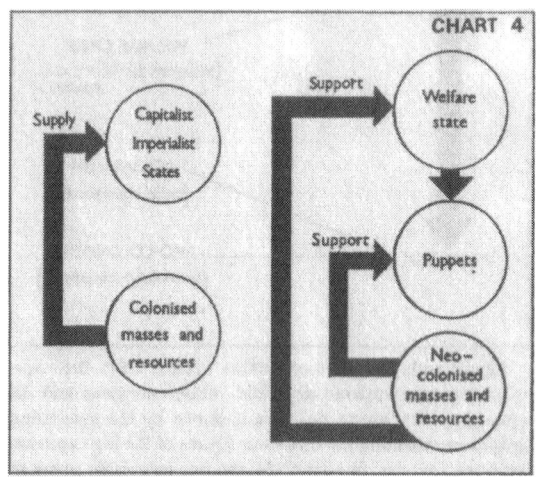

The explosive character of this situation cannot be denied. The neo-colonialist government is virtually in a state of permanent conflict with its own masses, whilst the gap between the puppet administration and neo-colonised workers widens every day.

- It is therefore clear that a puppet regime cannot draw its strength from the support of the broad masses. It can only stay in power as long as it manages to subsist in the teeth of popular opposition and revolt. Hence, the imperative need to depend on a foreign power for military assistance merely to keep the neo-colonised government physically in power.

Thus, the three essential components of neo-colonialism are :

1. Economic exploitation
2. Puppet governments and client states
3. Military assistance
4. Economic "aid"

The vital necessity of "military aid" is fulfilled through various channels : foreign technical assistance to the armed forces, control of the armed forces by officers and western military cadres, secret military agreements, the formation of special units for the repression of popular insurrection, and so on. The important thing is to know how to recognise this type of "aid", in whatever guise it appears, for it is the most blatant proof of the anti-popular, aggressive and basically violent character of all neo-colonialist regimes. Its escalation and impact increase proportionately to the widen- ing gap between the puppets and the oppressed masses, and it is directly related to the development of organised, popular resistance.

It is also to be noted that US policy found its most complete expression, after the murder of President Kennedy, in the Johnson doctrine whereby military aggres- sion, under the name of "preventive measures", became an integral part of neo-colonialist practice.

The struggle against neo-colonialism

Military strategy presupposes political aims. All military problems are political, and all political problems are economic.

Both the basic nature of neo-colonialism and the accu- mulated experience of liberation movements in Africa, Asia and Latin America indicate clearly that the only way for the broad masses to eradicate neo-colonialism is through a revolutionary movement springing from a direct confront- ation with the imperialists, and drawing its strength from the exploited and disinherited masses. The struggle against puppet governments, and against all forms of exploitation, is the basic condition for the survival and development of a genuine liberation movement in Africa. We must accept the challenge and fight to destroy this threat to our future as a free and united continent.

Independence must never be considered as an end in it- self but as a stage, the very first stage of the people's revo- lutionary struggle.

Propaganda and psychological warfare

Throughout the struggle we must recognise and combat enemy attempts to demoralise us. For, in the face of the failure to achieve military solutions against well-organised, broadly-based guerrilla forces, as for example in Vietnam, the enemy has stepped up its efforts in the propaganda war. The aim is:

To prevent a liberation movement from getting under way, by destroying it at its source, i.e. by undermining the will to fight.

Where revolutionary warfare has actually begun, to conquer it by political means, i.e. by granting just sufficient political, economic and social "reform" to encourage all but the so-called "extremists" to abandon the struggle.

Psychological attacks are made through the agency of broadcasting stations like the BBC, Voice of Germany, and above all, Voice of America, which pursues its brain- washing mission through newsreels, interviews and other "informative" programmes at all hours of the day and night, on all wavelengths and in many languages, including "special English". The war of words is supplemented by written propaganda using a wide range of political devices such as embassy bulletins, pseudo "revolutionary" publi- cations, studies on "nationalism" and on "African socia- lism", the literature spread by the so-called independent and liberal publishers, "cultural" and "civic education" centres, and other imperialist subversive organisations. The paper war penetrates into every town and village, and into the remotest parts of the "bush". It spreads in the form of free distributions of propaganda films praising the qualities of western civilisation and culture. These are some of the ways in which the psychological terrain is prepared. When the target, a certain country or continent, is suffi- ciently "softened", then the invasion of evangelist brigades begins, thus perpetuating the centuries old tactic whereby missionaries prepare the way for guns. Peace Corps divi- sions stream in, and Moral Rearmament units, Jehovah witnesses, information agencies and international financial "aid" organisations.

In this way, a territory or even an entire continent is besieged without a single marine in sight. A sprinkling of political and little-publicised murders, like that of Pio Pinto in Kenya, and Moumié in Geneva, are used to assist the process.

A recent development in the psychological war is the campaign to convince us that we cannot govern ourselves, that we are unworthy of genuine independence, and that foreign tutelage is the only remedy for our wild, warlike and primitive ways.

Imperialism has done its utmost to brainwash Africans into thinking that they need the strait-jackets of colonialism and neo-colonialism if they are to be saved from their retro- gressive instincts. Such is the age-old racialist justification for the economic exploitation of our continent. And now, the recent military coups engineered throughout Africa by foreign reactionaries are also being used to corroborate imperialism's pet theory that the Africans have shamelessly squandered the "golden opportunities" of independence, and that they have plunged their political kingdoms into blood and barbarism.

Therefore, the imperialist mission : we must save them anew; and they hail the western-trained and western-bought army puppets as saviours. The press, films and radio are fast spreading the myth of post-independence violence and chaos. Everywhere, the more or less covert implication is : Africa needs to be recolonised.

The fact that Africa has advanced politically more quickly than any other continent in the world is ignored. In 1957 when Ghana became independent and the political renaissance began in Africa, there were only eight inde- pendent states. Now, in just over ten years, there are over forty and the final liberation of the continent is in sight.

Imperialists are not content with trying to convince us that we are politically immature. They are telling us, now that we are realising that armed revolution is the only way to defeat neo-colonialism, that we are inherently incapable of fighting a successful revolutionary war.

This new psychological propaganda campaign is being waged in various subtle ways. First, there is what may be called the "moral" argument : Africans are constantly being reminded that they are a peace-loving, tolerant and communalist-minded people. The African is projected as an individual who has always been loath to shed blood. The corollary of this argument is that it would be immoral and against our nature to engage in revolutionary warfare.

The moral argument is easily destroyed. Centuries of liberation wars, wars of conquest, revolution and counter- revolution in the west were not considered to be moral or immoral. They were simply part of western historical development. **Our armed struggle for freedom is neither moral nor immoral, it is a scientific historically-determined necessity.**

The second argument used to deflect us from the inevi- tability of armed struggle is the so-called "economy" argu- ment. It runs something like this : modern neo-colonialism does not constitute a danger to young, revolutionary Afri- can states, and therefore the military training and arming of the broad masses is an expensive and frivolous enter- prise. The corollary of this reactionary argument is : since you cannot, in the present under-developed state of your economy, afford the "luxury" of your own defence, let us take care of it for you. And the trap is set.

Last but not least, is a third series of racialist and de- featist arguments designed to spread the myth that no Afri- can revolutionary is capable of carrying an armed struggle through to the end. It condemns a-priori all African revo- lutionary activities to failure. It wraps revolutionary war- fare on our continent in an aura of disparagement, and tries to cripple us with a sense of inadequacy as freedom fighters. By means of press and radio, accounts are given of the capture of "terrorists" by "security forces", (note the choice of words), the "terrorists" being usually described as poorly-trained, ill-equipped, demoralised and uncertain of the cause for which they are fighting. Where arms and military equipment are seized, it is always labelled "Russian" or "Chinese", to suggest that the freedom fighters who use them are not African nationalists, but the dupes and tools of foreign governments.

When freedom fighters are captured and tried in courts of law, they are treated as criminals, not as prisoners of war, and are imprisoned, shot or hanged, usually after so-called confessions have been extorted. This refusal to recognise freedom fighters as soldiers is again part of im- perialist strategy designed to pour scorn on the armed revo- lutionary movement, and at the same time to discourage further recruits.

The campaign is based on the counter-insurgency law whereby "it is necessary to attack the revolution during the initial stages of the movement when it is still weak, when it has not yet fulfilled that which should be its main aspiration,—a total integration with the people". (Ché Guevara.) This is why we are being told that Africans are incapable of sustaining revolutionary warfare : —
- a) racially
- b) because of our historical background
- c) for lack of cadres, ideology and leadership.

In one breath, we are accused of being too primitive to govern ourselves, and in the next we are accused of not being primitive enough to wage guerrilla warfare !

The problem is not whether one is born or is not born a natural revolutionary fighter. The problem is not whether revolutionaries are naturally suited to Africa, or Africa to revolutionary warfare. Predestination of this sort never exists. The fact is that revolutionary warfare is the key to African freedom and is the only way in which the total liberation and unity of the African continent can be achieved.

Foreign military preparedness

In pursuing their aggressive aims and fulfilling the re- quirements of military strategy, the imperialists have built up a system of military blocs and alliances which provide the framework for a pattern of military bases in strategically important positions all over the world. The African freedom fighters, while mainly concerned with enemy strength in Africa, must nevertheless study this world pattern if they are to assess correctly the true dimensions of their struggle. The anti-imperialist and neo-colonialist struggle will, in fact, be world-wide, since revolutionary warfare will occur wherever the enemy operates.

A substantial part of the military, anti-revolutionary effort is channelled into four organisations:

- NATO—North Atlantic Treaty Organisation (1949) USA, Britain, France, Italy, Belgium, Holland, Luxembourg, Canada, Iceland, Norway, Denmark, Portugal. Since October 1951 Greece and Turkey, and since 1954 West Germany.

- SEATO—South East Asia Treaty Organisation (1954) USA, Britain, France,

New Zealand, Australia, Philippines, Thailand and Pakistan.

- ANZUS—Australia, New Zealand, United States Treaty (1951). The Pacific Pact.

- CENTO—Central Treaty Organisation (1959)

- Britain, Turkey, Pakistan and Iran. Emerged from the 1955 Baghdad Pact. USA in 1959 entered into bilateral defence agreements with Turky, Iran and Pakistan.

In effect, this system of military blocs and alliances en- ables US imperialism to exert de facto leadership not only over the entire "western" world, but over extensive zones in Latin America and Asia. This is achieved through an external network of some 2,200 bases and installations manned by approximately a million troops in readiness for war.

The US external forces of intervention may be grouped as follows.

- Group One : Against the USSR with bases in Western Europe, North Africa and the Middle East.

- Group Two : Against China with bases in Pakistan, South East Asia and the Pacific Ocean.

- Group Three : Against revolutionary movements in Latin America—the Organisation of American States (OAS) group with bases in Panama, the Bermudas and Porto Rico.

In Africa, there are at present seventeen air bases owned and operated by members of

NATO. There are nine foreign naval bases. Foreign military missions exist for example in Kenya, Morocco, Liberia, Libya, South Africa, Senegal, Niger, Cameroon, Chad, Gabon and Ivory Coast. In addi- tion, there are three rocket sites and an atomic testing range in North Africa.

The armed forces of foreign powers in various strategi- cally-important parts of our continent present a serious threat but not an insurmountable obstacle in the African revolutionary struggle. For they must be assessed in con- junction with the forces of settler, minority governments in Rhodesia and South Africa, and with imperialist forces in the few remaining colonial territories.

The formation of NATO led to the signing of the Warsaw Treaty in 1954, by which the Soviet Union, Bulgaria, Hungary, German

Democratic Republic, Poland, Ru mania, Czechoslavakia and Albania made arrangements to protect themselves against imperialist aggression. An attack on any one member would be regarded as an attack on all. Provision was made for:
- a) A political consultative body to take political decisions and to exchange information
- b) A united military command with headquarters in Warsaw.

The need for Pan-African organisation

In comparison, the Independent States of Africa are at present militarily weak. Unlike the imperialists and neo- colonialists they have no mutual defence system and no unified command to plan and direct joint action. But this will be remedied with the formation of the All-African People's Revolutionary Army and the setting up of organi- sations to extend and plan effective revolutionary warfare on a continental scale.

We possess the vital ingredient necessary to win,—the full and enthusiastic support of the broad masses of the African people who are determined once and for all to end all forms of foreign exploitation, to manage their own affairs, and to determine their own future. Against such overwhelming strength organised on a Pan-African basis, no amount of enemy forces can hope to succeed.

Chapter Two
OUR OBJECTIVES

Our objectives are defined by the three political compo- nents of our liberation movement :
1. Nationalism
2. Pan-Africanism
3. Socialism

The three objectives of our struggle stem from our posi- tion as peoples in revolt against exploitation in Africa. These objectives are closely inter-related and one cannot be achieved fully without the other. If one of the three com- ponents is missing, no territory on our continent can secure genuine freedom or maintain a stable government.

Nationalism

Nationalism is the ideological channel of the anti-colonia- list struggle and represents the demand for national inde- pendence of colonised peoples. It is a concept most easily grasped by the population of territories where the low level of development of productive forces (and therefore of capi- talist implantation), and the absence of indigenous elements in the spheres of political power, are factors that facilitate the formation of a united militant front, one of the primary conditions for a successful liberation movement.

Colonised peoples are not highly differentiated from a social point of view, and are exploited practically without discrimination by the colonial power. Hence the slogan : "the nation must be freed from colonialism" is a univers ally accepted rallying cry whose influence is heightened by the fact that the agents of colonialism, exploiting the terri- tory from within, are there for everybody to see. It is there- fore the people as a whole who revolt and struggle as a "nation-class" against colonial oppression, and who win independence.

The nationalist phase is a necessary step in the liberation struggle, but must never be regarded as the final solution to the problem raised by the economic and political exploi- tation of our peoples. For nationalism is narrow in its appli- cation. It works within the geopolitical framework pro- duced by the colonial powers which culminated in the carve- up agreed upon in 1884 at the Berlin Conference, where today's political maps of Africa were drawn.

The various peoples of Africa cannot be, and historically never have been, confined behind rigid frontiers sealing off territories labelled "Nigeria", "Togo", "Senegal", and so on. The natural movements of the African peoples and of their societies have from time immemorial swept along extensive axes as for example from the Nile to the Congo, from Senegal to the Niger, and from the Congo to the Zambesi.

The African "nations" of today, created artificially by foreigners for their own purposes, neither originate from ancient African civilisation, nor do they fit in with our African way of life or habits of exchange. They are not even, for the most part, economically viable. Yet they continue to struggle on, each one separately, in a pathetic and hopeless attempt to make progress, while the real obstacle to their development, imperialism, mainly in its neo-colonialist stage, is operating on a Pan-African scale. Already, huge zones of Africa have been integrated eco- nomically in the exclusive interest of international finance capital. A study of the organisation and workings of most of the large trading firms, mining trusts and industrial cartels operating in Africa shows that they all function directly or indirectly on a continental scale. Many of them form part of a general network spreading over several continents.

This monopolistic system of exploitation is the direct outcome of prolonged capitalist practice, the experience being that extended and unified industrial, commercial or mining units are less costly to maintain, are more efficient, and produce higher profits.

It is time that we also planned our economic and political development on a continental scale. The concept of African unity embraces the fundamental needs and characteristics of African civilisation and ideology, and at the same time satis- fies all the conditions necessary for an accelerated economic and technological advance. Such maximum development would ensure a rational utilisation of the material resources and human potential of our continent along the lines of an integrated economy, and within complementary sectors of production, eliminating all unnecessary forms of competi- tion, economic alienation and duplication. The idea is not to destroy or dismantle the network of foreign mining com- plexes and industrial companies throughout Africa, but to take them over and operate them in the sole interest of the African peoples.

Finally, the limitations of "nationalism" may be seen in the experience of countries which have succeeded in casting off one imperialism only to be oppressed by another, or by a syndicate of imperialisms, as in Latin America. Merely to change masters is no solution to colonial poverty or neo- colonialist strangulation, even if exploitation is subsequently practised in a more subtle way.

African unity gives an indispensable continental dimension to the concept of the African nation.

Pan-Africanism

The limitations of nationalism have already been acknow- ledged by the most mature leaders of the liberation move- ment; but wherever the conditions for the transition to a higher ideological level and a wider form of struggle were lacking, the necessary leap could not be made, and nationa- lism was never transcended.

The true dimensions of our struggle were outlined at the Fifth Pan-African Congress held in Manchester, England in 1945, when resolutions were passed specifying that the supreme objective of the national liberation movement was to pave the way to national reconstruction and to promote democracy and prosperity for the broad masses through an All-African struggle against colonialism and all the new manifestations of imperialism No reference was made to neo-colonialism as such, because this only developed on a massive scale in Africa after 1957. But the Pan-Africanism which found expression at the Manchester Congress (1945), and the All-African People's Conference (1958) was based on the age-old aspiration towards unity of all peoples of African origin exploited as workers and as a race.

African unity therefore implies:
1. **That imperialism and foreign oppression should be eradicated in all their forms.**
2. **That neo-colonialism should be recognised and elimi- nated.**
3. **That the new African nation must develop within a continental framework.**

However, the specific content of the new social order within the developing African nation remains to be defined.

Socialism

At the core of the concept of African unity lies socialism and the socialist definition of the new African society.

Socialism and African unity are organically complementary.

Socialism implies:

1. Common ownership of the means of production, dis- tribution and exchange. Production is for use, and not for profit.
2. Planned methods of production by the state, based on modern industry and agriculture.
3. Political power in the hands of the people, with the entire body of workers possessing the necessary gov- ernmental machinery through which to express their needs and aspirations. It is a concept in keeping with the humanist and egalitarian spirit which character- ised traditional African society, though it must be applied in a modern context. All are workers; and no person exploits another.
4. Application of scientific methods in all spheres of thought and production.

Socialism must provide a new social synthesis in which the advanced technical society is achieved without the appalling evils and deep cleavages of capitalist industrial society.

Socialism has become a necessity in the platform diction of African political leaders, though not all pursue really socialist policies. We must therefore be on our guard against measures which are declared to be "socialist" but which do not in fact promote economic and social development. An example of muddled thinking about socialism is the attempt made in recent years to suggest the existence of an "African Socialism" peculiar to our continent.

There is only one true socialism and that is scientific socialism, the principles of which are abiding and universal. The only way to achieve it is to devise policies aimed at general socialist goals, which take their form from the con- crete, specific circumstances and conditions of a particular country at a definite historical period.

The socialist countries of Africa may differ in the details of their policies. There are different paths to socialism, and adjustments have to be made to suit particular circumstances. But they should not be arbitrarily decided, or sub- ject to vagaries of taste. They must be scientifically explained.

Only under socialism can we reliably accumulate the capital we need for our development, ensure that the gains of investment are applied to the general welfare, and achieve our goal of a free and united continent.

The present stage of the liberation struggle

An objective appraisal of the degree of success so far attained in our struggle leads to the consideration of three theses of major importance :
1. The achievement of genuine independence by an African state is but a part of the over-all process of continental decolonisation.
2. No independent state is immune to imperialist in- trigue, pressure and subversion as long as imperialism under any guise is left free to operate on the African continent.
3. The degree of completeness of our victory over im- perialism has a determining influence on how far post- independence reconstruction can go. In other words, **the**

people will have no equitable share in national reconstruction and its benefits unless the victory over imperialism in its colonialist and neo-colonialist stages is complete.

It therefore follows that the unity of the African people expressed in a Union Government is necessary :
- a) to accelerate the liberation struggle in territories still under colonial domination.
- b) for the security of already independent states, and particularly for those which have chosen to follow a line of total opposition to imperialism.
- c) to protect the flanks of our drive towards socialist, domestic reconstruction.

These considerations should be able to serve as :

a. A basic formula to link up with all aspects of the anti- imperialist struggle in Africa.
b. A blue-print for the people's action.
c. A yardstick for the evaluation of political develop- ment and phases in the history of Africa.

Accumulated experience of the African People's unity movement Equipped with a clear knowledge of our objectives, we are in a position to undertake a critical appraisal of recent developments in African history. This is necessary if we are to draw positive lessons from past experience, to deter- mine both the area of deviation and the need for correction, and to devise a more effective strategy for the future.

Shortly after Ghana achieved independence in 1957 there began a rapid succession of events caused by a great up- surge of interest in the African people's movement towards emancipation and unity. The three most significant events which sparked off the process were :

1. The first Conference of Independent African States held in Accra in April 1958. At that time there were only eight independent states : Ethiopia, Ghana, Liberia, Libya, Morocco, Sudan, Tunisia and Egypt. The purpose was to :
   a) discuss questions of mutual interest
   b) explore ways and means of consolidating and safeguarding independence
   c) strengthen the economic and cultural ties between the independent states
   d) find ways of helping Africans still oppressed under colonial rule.

The African leaders in attendance were resolutely and unanimously anti-imperialist, and agreed to co-ordinate diplomacy, mainly at UN level.

Pan-African conferences had hitherto been held over- seas. In 1958, Pan-Africanism had moved to the African continent, where it really belonged.

2. The All-African Peoples' Conference held in Accra in December 1958. Representatives of sixty-two African nationalist organisations attended and dis-cussed the various aspects of the liberation movement. The organisation of unitary action between African political movements was then launched.
3. The third All-African Peoples' Conference held in Cairo in March 1961, when the whole question of neo-colonialism was brought to the forefront in discus- sions on the African revolutionary struggle.

The development of unitary, anti-imperialist action be- tween struggling peoples, and at the level of the governments of independent

states, constituted a two-pronged attack against imperialism.
The imperialists acted accordingly :

a) through diplomatic pressure
b) by granting sham independence to a number of states.

The trick worked well. However, a clear prefiguration of later events was to be enacted at the Sanniquellie Conference held in Liberia in July 1959. Two views were expressed on the question of African unity. The first advocated the tightest "binding together of our forces in political unity", while the second was in favour of a "formula flexible enough to enable each state to safeguard its national sovereignty and personal identity".

The latter view fitted in only too well with the objectives of the imperialists who had already recognised the need to adapt their policies to the changing colonial situation.

Hard pressed by the armed struggle of the FLN in Algeria and to avoid any further crystallisation of revolutionary awareness amongst "extremist" African leaders, they decided to play their own version of nationalism.

Accordingly, between 1959 and 1960, thirteen indepen- dent states emerged : eleven former French colonies, and Congo-Leopoldville and Nigeria. A close analysis of the specific conditions under which each one of the thirteen states became independent reveals that neo-colonialism was incipient during the movement for independence, and emerged fully once independence was acquired.

Sham independence and the unity movement

Few were deceived by such a deliberate and obvious stratagem. Imperialism was merely using the device of sham independence to prepare the African terrain to suit its own convenience, and to avoid a direct and costly confrontation with the liberation movements.

It was therefore not surprising that the divisions of opinion on the question of unity expressed at Sanniquellie, were much more in evidence during the Second Conference of Independent African States held in Addis Ababa in 1960. At this Conference :
1. The pivot of African unity was seen no longer as a firm political union, but merely as a loose policy of co-operation between African states. Moreover, the concept of regional groupings between states was endorsed.
2. The principle of a collective foreign policy as agreed upon in Accra in 1958 gave way to the principle of a separate foreign policy for each state. In this way, imperialists gained more room for manoeuvre, for infiltration

and for stirring up difficulties between African states.
3. It was agreed that assistance to the Algerian liberation struggle was to take the form of diplomatic pressure on France, but was to by-pass official recognition of the GPRA.* In plain words, diplomatic shilly-shallying was to take the place of a genuine anti-imperialist confrontation.

Therefore, as early as 1960, a wide gulf developed between those independent states which favoured co-operation with imperialism, and those which proclaimed an unflinching offensive against it.

The emergence of conflicting trends was not fortuitous but a logical consequence of the state of tension between qualitatively different situations :
1. **Genuine independence,** the product of a mass politi- cal

movement or an armed liberation struggle.
2. **Sham independence,** established by imperialists in an attempt to arrest the progress of the people's move- ment through a betrayal of its essential objectives.

*Algerian Provisional Government

It is important to note that it was not the moderate policy of co-operation with imperialism which created the "mod- erate" African states. On the contrary, it was the deliberate creation of such states by imperialism which gave rise to moderation and co-operation. The will to compromise is but a reflection, at diplomatic level of the neo-colonialist character of certain African states; it is the external mani- festation of the inner characteristics of neo-colonial regimes.

African people's wars and imperialist escalation

However, far from weakening the anti-imperialist struggle and the vanguard revolutionary states, such measures can only strengthen their vigilance and revolutionary deter- mination.

Since 1960, the struggle of the African people and the more or less latent state of crisis inside many African terri- tories have reached maturity. To counter-balance the growing revolutionary character of the African situation, the enemy's reaction has become more open and direct. Both the Algerian and the Congolese wars were born of the people's determination to free themselves at whatever cost, the only difference being that the Algerian revolt developed in an essentially colonial context, whereas the Congolese struggle is being waged in a neo-colonialist setting, marked by major imperialist aggression throughout the African continent.

From a practical point of view, the differences between the various segments of the liberation struggle in time and space are minimal. The only factors which render the Congolese, Angolese or Rhodesian struggles (to take these examples only) more violent than others are, first, the escalation of imperialist action; and secondly, the more advanced nature of the people's organisation, though the actual level of readiness to revolt may be just as high else- where.

Significantly, it was the frenzy of imperialist repression against the Algerian and Congolese liberation struggles which led to the calling of the Casablanca Conference in 1961, to which the GPRA was invited. The "Casablanca" states, as they were subsequently named, (i.e. Ghana, Guinea, Mali, Libya, Egypt, Morocco), and the Algerian FLN called for decisive action on the part of the independent states to support the anti-imperialist struggle in Africa. Further, a strong appeal for unity was made. For **"in unity lies strength. African states must unite or sell themselves out to imperialist and colonialist exploiters for a mess of pottage, or disintegrate individually"**.

Meantime, two new groupings, alike in content and with similar policies, were being formed :
1. The Monrovia group which met in Monrovia in May 1961 consisting mainly of English-speaking states whose loyalties were basically Anglo-American.
2. The Brazzaville group made up of French-speaking states mostly aligned to France.

Both these groups adopted a "go slow" attitude towards African emancipation and unity, and pursued a policy of conciliation with imperialism. Their views were expressed at the Lagos Conference (January 1962) when twenty of Africa's twenty-eight independent states met to discuss ways in which co-operation could be achieved. They agreed that :

a) The absolute sovereignty and legality of each African state must be respected.
b) The union of one state with another should be effected on a voluntary basis.
c) There should be non-interference in each other's affairs.
d) Political refugees from one state should not be given asylum in another state.

North Africa was unrepresented at the Lagos Confer- ence because the Algerian Provisional Government was not invited.

The Casablanca powers and the Sudan also declined to go for the same reason.

Imperialist diplomacy appeared to have achieved its purpose admirably, in splitting up the independent states of Africa into separate and conflicting groups. The efforts of the militant Casablanca group were checked by a pro- imperialist bloc, which was in its turn sub-divided into pro-French and pro-English branches.

The Organisation of African Unity (OAU)

The militant African forces did achieve a certain amount of success when all blocs and groups joined together to form the OAU at Addis Ababa in 1963. However, appearances are sometimes deceptive: the dissolution of pro-imperialist groups did not mean that the interests they represented had also vanished.

On the contrary, an examination of recent events exposes serious weaknesses within the OAU. The Organisation failed to solve the crises in the Congo and Rhodesia : both of them test cases,—the former involving a direct challenge to neo-colonialism, and the latter open confrontation with a minority, settler government. In fact, the OAU is in danger of developing into a useful cover for the continued, sterile action of conflicting interests, the only difference being, that in the context of one big "brotherly" organisation reactionary tactics are camouflaged and applied through the subleties of negotiation.

This change of tactics works as strongly as ever against the fundamental interests of progressive forces in Africa, since it hides concessions to imperialism.

Negotiations are conducted behind closed doors and sur- rounded by a mysterious cloak of diplomatic protocol, making knowledge of the proceedings inaccessible to the general public.

However, four explosive issues discussed at the OAU Conference in Accra in 1965, alerted progressive opinion to the dangers of continued compromise :
1. The crisis in Rhodesia.
2. The struggle in the Congo.
3. The treatment of African political refugees.
4. The problem of South West Africa.

In the first case, the African heads of state failed to agree on a practical way of checking Ian Smith's rebellion, and instead fell back on the futile policy of negotiations with Britain combined with diplomatic pressure at international and UN level.

Similarly, in the Congo, the fundamental issue of the crisis was avoided in spite of the tense situation resulting from the gallant stand of the freedom fighters carrying on the struggle in the spirit of Lumumba.

On the question of the status and treatment of African political refugees the OAU again failed to find a solution, and heads of state continued to regard them merely as outlaws or barter-goods.

The radical African states in the OAU were confronted with the difficulty of finding effective expression for the aspirations of the broad masses of the people. The struggle seemed to unfold in two different spheres : the one in the streets, villages, workshops and factories; and the other in the hushed and closed atmosphere of air-conditioned houses and offices. In this situation the genuine threat of imperia- lism and its neo-colonialist agents tended to be under-estimated, and the progressive states placed too much reliance on the OAU.

In the meantime, the pro-imperialist states, although pretending to rally to the revolutionary elements within the OAU in order to avoid a direct confrontation, had been creating and expanding an organisation after their own heart : the Organisation Commune Africaine et Malgache (OCAM), into a larger unit to include all French-speaking African states under the name "Francophonie". As a result, the progressive states, failing to close their ranks, were left to fight inadequately and alone against the massive escalation of imperialism, and the active consolida- tion of its position through plots and a series of coups d'état.

Some essential features of the enemy's offensive

1. Externally

Mounting imperialist aggression in Africa foreshadows a decline in the strength of imperialism since the use of violence to maintain imperialist rule invariably sparks off a stronger explosion of revolutionary activity among op- pressed peoples, and experience has shown that such move- ments can be neither destroyed nor contained. The Ameri- can fiascos in Vietnam, Santo Domingo and Cuba illustrate the point. So, also do the resolutions condemning US imperialism passed by representatives from three continents (Africa, Asia and Latin America) when they met in con- ference at Havana in 1966. Taken aback by the compelling reality of tri-continental solidarity, the US imperialists hastened to condemn the Havana resolutions as "subver- sive" and resolved to take "appropriate preventive meas- ures, including military action" against any popular move- ment considered to be a danger to the "free world" under US leadership. At the same time, they predicted other coups in Africa during the ensuing year, and immediately set to work, with or without the collaboration of European accomplices, to help this prediction to come true.

It was evidently felt that the resort to quick action was necessary because of the uncompromising stand against imperialist action in the "hot" zones of the world, taken by progressive governments. The latter were succeeding in arousing world opinion against imperialist atrocities in Vietnam, and in drawing attention to the worsening crises in Rhodesia and the Congo, the South African military build up, NATO's assistance to Portugal in her colonial wars, and "interventions" in Latin America and the Caribbean.

2. Internally

The capitalist imperialist states face serious economic and social difficulties. Rising prices, balance of payments problems, widespread and repeated strikes are only a few of the symptoms of the general malaise. In the United States, the grave domestic situation is aggravated by the massive counter-attacks of the African-American revolutionaries.

Almost everywhere, behind the smoke screens, the social and economic situation is unhealthy, and particularly in the second class capitalist states. And these mounting economic crises mean heavier and heavier dependence on the exploitation of the peoples of Africa, Asia and Latin America.

The need for self-critical objective diagnosis

If imperialists are faced with so many external and dom- estic difficulties, how then can they afford to step up their aggression in Africa? To answer this question, it is necessary to examine the internal factors which make our continent so vulnerable to attack, and particularly to look closely at the whole question of African unity. For this lies at the core of our problem.

There are three conflicting conceptions of African unity which explain to a large extent, the present critical situation in Africa :

1. **The mutual protection theory:** that the OAU serves as a kind of insurance against any change in the status quo, membership providing a protection for heads of state and government against all forms of political action aimed at their overthrow. Since most of the leaders who adhere to this idea owe

their position to imperialists and their agents, it is not surprising that this is the viewpoint which really serves the interests of imperialism. For the puppet states are being used both for short-term purposes of exploitation and as spring-boards of subversion against progressive African states.

2. **The functional conception:** that African unity should be purely a matter of economic co-operation. Those who hold this view overlook the vital fact that Afri- can regional economic organisations will remain weak and subject to the same neo-colonialist pressures and domination, as long as they lack overall political cohesion. Without political unity, African states can never commit themselves to **full** economic integration, which is the only productive form of integration able to develop our great resources fully for

the well-being of the African people as a whole. Furthermore, the lack of political unity places inter- African economic institutions at the mercy of power- ful, foreign commercial interests, and sooner or later these will use such institutions as funnels through which to pour money for the continued exploitation of Africa.

3. **The Political Union Conception:** that a union government should be in charge of economic development, defence and foreign policy, while other government functions would continue to be discharged by the existing states grouped, in federal fashion, within a gigantic central political organisation.

Clearly, this is the strongest position Africa could adopt in its struggle against modern imperialism.

However, any sincere critical appraisal of past activities and achievements of the OAU would tend to show that, as it is now constituted, the OAU is not likely to be able to achieve the political unification of Africa.

This is obviously why imperialists, although against the idea of political union, will do nothing to break the OAU. It serves their purpose in slowing down revolutionary progress in Africa. This state of affairs is mirrored both in the discouragement of freedom fighters in the remaining colonial territories and South Africa, and in the growing perplexity amongst freedom fighters from neo-colonised territories.

The struggle for African continental union and socialism may be hampered by the enemy within,those who declare their support for the revolution and at the same time, by devious means, serve and promote the interests of imperialists and neo-colonialists.

Examination of recent events in our history, and of our present condition, reveals the urgent need for a new strategy to combat imperialist aggression, and this must be devised on a continental scale.

Either we concentrate our forces for a decisive armed struggle to achieve our objectives, or we will each fall one by one to the blows of imperialism in its present stage of and desperate offensive.

BOOK TWO

STRATEGY, TACTICS AND TECHNIQUES

PREFACE

Revolutionary warfare is the logical, inevitable answer to the political, economic and social situation in Africa today. We do not have the luxury of an alternative . We are faced with a necessity.

Throughout the world, the escalation of imperialist aggression is making the issues clear, and exploitation can no longer be disguised. In Africa, a point of explosion against imperialism has been reached. But only a massive and organised will to fight can spark it off.

Time is running out. We must act now. The freedom fighters already operating in many parts of Africa must no longer be allowed to bear the full brunt of a continental struggle against a continental enemy. The collective and continental nature of our will and our space, the urgency of conquering the initiative and the protracted nature of a revolutionary war calls for a united All-African organisation of all freedom fighters on the African continent.

We must co-ordinate strategy and tactics, and combine experience. Co-ordination requires organisation, and organisation can only be effective if each fighting unit is a disciplined part of the whole. Attack must be planned with diversion, retreat with consolidation, losses in one zone compensated for by gains in another, until the liberation movement is finally victorious, and the whole of Africa is free and united.

As a continental nation we are young, strong and resilient. The cohesive planning of our struggle and the combined strength of our will to win will do the rest.

Africa is one; and this battle must be fought and won continentally.

Chapter One

ORGANISATION FOR REVOLUTIONARY WARFARE

A. THE MILITARY BALANCE

The dimension of our struggle is equal to the size of the African continent itself. It is in no way confined within any of the absurd limits of the micro-states created by the colonial powers, and jealously guarded by imperialist puppets during the neo-colonialist period.

For although the African nation is at present split up among many separate states, it is in reality simply divided into two : our enemy and ourselves. The strategy of our struggle must be determined accordingly, and our conti- nental territory considered as consisting of three categories of territories which correspond to the varying levels of popular organisation and to the precise measure of victory attained by the people's forces over the enemy :

1. Liberated areas
2. Zones under enemy control
3. Contested zones (i.e. hot points).

Liberated Areas

These areas may present minimal differences due to the varying ways in which independence was obtained. However, they can be collectively defined as territories where :

a) Independence was secured through an armed struggle, or through a positive action movement represent- ing the majority of the population under the leader- ship of an anti-imperialist and well-organised mass party.

b) A puppet regime was overthrown by a people's movement (Zanzibar, Congo-Brazzaville, Egypt).

c) A social revolution is taking place to consolidate political independence by:
   1. promoting accelerated economic development
   2. improving working conditions
   3. establishing complete freedom from dependence on foreign economic interests.

It therefore follows that a liberated zone can only be organised by a radically anti-imperialist party whose duty it is :

a) to decolonise, and

b) to teach the theory and practice of socialism as app- lied to the African social milieu, and adapted to local circumstances.

The people's socialist parties take the necessary steps to transform the united but heterogeneous front which fought for independence into an ideologically monolithic party of cadres.

Thus, in a truly liberated territory, one can observe :

1. Political growth achieved as a result of discussions and agreements concluded within the party.

2. Steady progress to transform theory into practice along the ideological lines drawn by the party.
3. Constant improvement, checking and re-checking of the development plans to be carried out by the party and at state level.
4. Political maturity among party members, who are nolonger content to follow a vague and general line of action. Revolutionary political maturity is the pre- lude to the re-organisation of the party structure along more radical lines.

However, no territory may be said to be truly liberated if the party leadership, apart from consolidating the gains of national independence does not also undertake to :

a) Support actively the detachments of revolutionary liberation movements in the contested zones of Africa.

b) Contribute to the organisation and revolutionary practice of the people's forces in neo-colonialist states,
c) i.e. in zones under enemy control or in contested areas.

d) Effect an organic liaison of its political and economic life with the other liberated zones of the African nation.

This implies a system of mutual servicing and aid be- tween the various detachments of the liberation movements and the liberated zones, so that a continuous exchange of experience, advice and ideas will link the progressive parties in power with the parties struggling in the contested zones. Each liberated zone should be ready to offer the use of its territory to detachments of the liberation movements so that the latter may establish their rear bases on friendly soil, and benefit from the provision of communications, hospitals, schools, factories, workshops, etc.

It is important to bear in mind that a liberated area is constantly exposed to the many forms of enemy action and attack. It is the duty of both the liberation movements and the liberated zones :

To make objective and up-to-date analyses of the enemy's aggression.

To base lost to the enemy and to help correct the mistakes which enabled the enemy to gain temporary victory.

In fact, the liberated areas of Africa do not yet come fully up to all the standards required of them. For example, in certain liberated zones, the level of economic liberation is clearly inferior to the high level of revolutionary awareness. But the main criterion for judging them to be liberated is the actual direction in which they are moving, since our assessment is of changing, not static phenomena.

Zones under enemy control

The imperialists control such zones:

a) through an administration manned by foreigners. The territory is then externally subjected.

b) through a puppet government made up of local ele- ments. The territory is then both internally and ex- ternally subjected.

c) through a settler, minority government. In this territory, settlers have established the rule of a majority by a minority. There is no logic except the right of might that can accept such a situation. **The predominant racial group must, and will, provide the govern- ment of a country. Settlers, provided they accept the principle of one man one vote, and majority rule, may be tolerated; but settler minority governments, never. They are a dangerous anachronism, and must be swept away completely and for ever.**

A territory under enemy control therefore is governed against the interests of the majority. Such zones are eco- nomically, militarily and politically alienated. It is precisely in these territories that the enemy has its military camps, aerodromes, naval establishments and broadcasting stations, and where foreign banks, insurance firms, mining, industrial and trading companies have their headquarters. In other words, these zones are enemy nerve centres.

Clear proof of the neo-colonialist and neo-liberated character of these states is seen in the refusal of their governments to allow liberation movements to open offices, establish bases or enjoy freedom of transit for troops and equipment on their way to the front.

The strength of a territory under enemy control may be assessed by taking into account the following factors :

I. the level of organisation attained by the reactionary forces in control there

II. the type and degree of repression exerted against the people's liberation movement

III. the degree and modes of exploitation exerted upon the toiling masses

IV. the military means available to the reactionaries in power

V. the nature of the economic interests imperialism is out to promote in that territory and in neighbouring areas, (for example, strategic materials, important commercial and industrial complexes etc.)

VI. the over-all strategic advantages which imperialism hopes to gain from the subjugation of the territory. Such gains may be exclusively political.

As far as our struggle is concerned, our most vital asset is the degree of revolutionary awareness attained by the workers and the masses in the zone under enemy control.

The political maturity or immaturity of the masses con- stitutes the main difference between an enemy-held zone and a contested zone.

The revolutionary awareness of the broad masses in an enemy-held zone, must express itself in national boycotts, strikes, sabotage and insurrection.

It would be a mistake to maintain that the total of areas under enemy control is exactly equal to the sum of neo- colonialist and colonialist governments. Socio-political phenomena are less mechanical than that. In each case it is the level of the people's awareness and participation that counts.

Contested zones

A zone under enemy control can at any time become a contested area if the revolutionary forces in activity there are either on the verge of armed struggle or have reached an advanced stage of revolutionary organisation. In some cases, a spark is enough to determine the turning point from preparation to action. In other circumstances, the embers can smoulder underground for a much longer period.

"Sham independence" zones, where the awakened masses have placed the enemy in such a precarious posi- tion that a "single spark can start a prairie fire", can no longer be said to be "under enemy control". In such a situation, the enemy is only superficially in command, and relies exclusively on support in the police, civil service and the army, where it retains control only as long as the force of habit remains unchallenged. It is to be noted that the army and police are never homogeneous forces in Africa, and that this factor is of obvious tactical interest in a revo- lutionary struggle primarily based on the workers and peasants, but also aiming to obtain the support of all other possible elements.

In these zones of revolutionary transition, the population feels deeply in sympathy with the revolutionary forces in neighbouring areas, and often gives them invaluable assistance.

These transitional zones may :

1. Either be used to organise the liberaton of another neighbouring territory which is economically more important and politically more mature, (for instance, where a party of revolutionary opposition is already operating against the government).

2. Or, in case of strategic necessity, be directly seized from the enemy through the organisation and armed action of the dissatisfied masses.

A careful study should be made of the range of possibili- ties offered by a territory under puppet, neo-colonialist control. Full investigation will disclose that the puppet government is not homogeneous, and that it is therefore vulnerable. It will also be found that the people are often virtually liberated but that they are not aware of it because no one has organised them to act purposefully to seize what is their due (i.e. political control and the control of economic wealth).

Between a zone under enemy control where the masses are awakening and a hotly-contested zone, there is only one missing link: a handful of genuine revolutionaries prepared to organise and act.

There are many more contested zones than liberated ones. In fact, the total area of contested zones covers most of the African continent. All the more reason why we should take vigilant care of our liberated territories.

A contested zone is not only a zone of revolutionary activity, but it is also an area in which a people's party works underground or semi-clandestinely to organise the over- throw of a puppet government. For there is no fundamental difference between armed struggle as such and organised revolutionary action of a civil type. The various methods of our struggle, and the changing from one method to another should be determined mainly by the circumstances and the set of conditions prevailing in a given territory.

The forces struggling in the contested zones are in the front line of the revolutionary liberation movement. They must receive material support from the liberated zones in order to carry their mission through to a successful end. This involves a development of the struggle until a people's insurrectionary movement is able to assume power.

A political party operating in a contested zone may be said to be truly revolutionary if :

1. It is actively organising the people, training cadres, etc.

2. Its essential objective is the total destruction of the puppet government or the colonial power, in order to build in its place the organs of the people's political power based on mass organisation and mass education.

The latter objective can only be achieved through a policy of direct confrontation with the enemy, and not through devious negotiations and compromise. This is the only correct approach to the African situation if the problem of the revolution is to be studied in depth and from the people's point of view.

Retarding Factors

However, certain factors have retarded the final un- leashing of anti-imperialist action and the unfolding of a people's revolution throughout the African nation :

1. The readiness of imperialists to exploit any cracks in our armour.

2. The undue emphasis placed on diplomatic procedure and negotiations to provide solutions.

3. The varying degrees of isolationism practised by the cadres of ruling parties in spite of their recognition,on a theoretical level, of the necessity for a

continental, anti-imperialist struggle and reconstruction.

4. The tendency manifested by certain ruling parties in the liberated zones to indulge in a slack, wait-andsee policy, merely toying with progressive ideas, and neglecting to analyse, handle and resolve national problems in a positive way. This has created a dangerous climate of uneasiness, confusion and discouragement for African revolutionaries, and fertile ground for neo-colonialist intrigue and attacks.

5. The existence of a more or less conscious opportunism amongst some leaders of the liberation movement both in the liberated and contested territories, which is symptomatic of a low level of ideological conviction.

High Command

Africa will he liberated sooner or later against all odds. But if it is to be soon, by an accelerated revolution of the people, and a total war against imperialism, then we must establish a unified continental high command here and now, to plan revolutionary war, and to initiate action.

If we fail to do this, and to lead the people's revolution, we are likely to be swept away one by one by imperialism and neo-colonialism. It is no longer feasible to take a middle course. The time for reform, however progressive, is past. For reforms cannot hold the enemy at bay, nor can they convince the silent, internal agents of neo-colonialism, eliminate the puppets, or even destroy the capitalist structure and mentality inherited from colonialism. The cancerous growths are proliferating at the very heart of our parties and territories whether they emerge under the cloak of constitutionalism, parliamentarianism, bureaucratic etiquette, an imposing civil service, officers trained in western "a- political" tradition to maintain the bourgeois-capitalist status quo by means of military coups, or if they appear in the more obvious guise of corruption and nepotism.

The people's armed struggle, the highest form of poli- tical action, is a revolutionary catalyst in the neo-colonialist situation.

Peaceful political action to achieve liberation has been proved ineffective

a) with the accession of the majority of African states to independence and the advent of neo-colonialism on a massive scale

b) with the increasingly continental dimension of our struggle.

Pacific political action was, in general, potent during the national phase of the liberation movement, and mainly in sub-Saharan Africa, where independence often developed in a chain reaction. However, even then there were signifi- cant exceptions. In Kenya for example, where recourse to peaceful political action was denied to the masses, the people's movement resorted to more direct and concentrated action in the form of Mau Mau. In Algeria, a seven year armed liberation struggle was needed. Elsewhere, the in- dependence movement pushed beyond the fringe of paci- ficism, as in Ghana and Guinea where "positive action" was employed.

I. The crystallisation of a more concentrated form of poli- tical action is in fact to be found in the development of almost all African independence movements. The reason for this was the need to establish a new social order after nomi- nal independence has been achieved, and the escalation of imperialist action. The latter appeared in :

II. the corruption of independence through neo-colonial- ism and puppet regimes.

III. direct imperialist aggression against liberation forces, for example in the Congo.

   a) increased multilateral and bilateral imperialist support to :

   b) remaining colonial powers (Portugal, Spain)

   c) fascist-racist regimes (Rhodesia, South Africa) puppet regimes and local reactionaries to assist their infiltration and attempts to suppress progressive and revolutionary forces throughout the continent.

In less than three years, from 1960, the armed form of struggle became a necessity of the African anti-colonial liberation movement, and the same process may he ob- served in most neo-colonialist situations.

From 1961 onwards, the armed form of political action reached another turning point with the creation of a united front co-ordinating the struggle of freedom fighters in all the "Portuguese" colonies. This organisation (CONCP) links up the politico-military struggle of 12,400,000 inhabitants over an area of some 2 million square kilometres.

In effect, then, anti-imperialist pacifism is dying, and on a continental scale, because :

I. The political action which led to independence devi- ated to become the sole monopoly and privilege of a reactionary "élite" which deprives the masses of the right to political action, even in its pacific and constitutional form.

II. Neo-colonialism has created a situation whereby the masses are exploited beyond the "safe" limits of exploitation.

The ensuing massive explosion of pent-up discontent can be nothing but violent. The masses seize back their right to political action and make maximum use of it.

3. Imperialist action is escalating

(a) to consolidate its positions (military coups d'état in neo-colonialist states).

(b) to gain ground and recapture lost initiative (reactionary
coups d'état in progressive states).

4. Imperialism constantly infiltrates revolutionary opposition
groups with agents, "special police", and others, compelling such groups to arm even before they have attained the organisational stage of armed struggle.

5. Whenever the pseudo-democratic institutions inherited
from colonial rule are not used by its inheritors to build capitalism but are gradually remodelled or
suddenly re-structured towards a socialist line of development, imperialists intervene violently.

6. Violence clears the "neo-colonialist fog" and reveals the invisible enemy and the subtle methods of camouflage

employed by neo-colonialists. The issues are made clear.

As soon as the initial revolutionary units emerge, the puppet regime is doomed. A chain reaction begins. The puppets are compelled to break the promises they have made. They had survived in the teeth of opposition only because they uneasily preserved an outward appearance of progressive action. Now, they have to suppress and kill openly in order to survive. Once the first drop of patriotic blood is shed in
the fight the puppet regime is irrevocably condemned.

Guerrilla points spread like oil stains. Not only have theinternal contradictions of neo-colonialism fully ripened
but the African masses have attained such a degree of poli- tical awareness that they literally force the struggle to break out into the open.

The Need for Co-ordinated Revolutionary Action

The international balance of forces, and more particularly the existence of powerful socialist states, gave rise to the theory that in certain territories dominated by imperialism on our continent it was possible to take a pacific road to socialism. But such reasoning is based on the false premise that the question of coordinating revolutionary action in Africa and the world has already been solved and that therefore imperialism is no longer able to concentrate its forces to act decisively against the most threatening parts of the popular liberation front.

In reality, the situation is quite different :

1. Imperialists are waging an all-out struggle against the socialist states,

and the revolutionary liberation movements through military means, and through insidious but powerful methods of psychological warfare (propaganda).

2. Imperialists have formed an international syndicate of military and economic forces to achieve its aggressive aims.

3. Imperialists have, in recent years, assisted in the establishment of numerous puppet governments in Africa.

The historical experience of the people of Asia, Latin America and of Africa has shown that imperialism has often forcefully intervened to prevent the peaceful achievement of socialism. In the case of Ghana a coup occurred at the very time a decisive turning point in socialist development was about to be reached.

The continental scope now attained by popular insurrection in Africa is a reality. It remains for us to devise effective co-ordinating machinery.

Our accumulated experience has shown that only practical and planned co-ordination on a continental scale will prevent the enemy from concentrating its forces on isolated and therefore more vulnerable targets. In our war, isolation is one of the greatest dangers.

We have already been able to outpace the enemy in certain ways by :

1. increasing our means or production

2. bringing a higher level of organisation to the people

3. spreading the essential features of the African people's revolution

4. unmasking neo-colonialism and its puppets.

We have succeeded in accummulating energy and will- power. But it is also true that we have not yet defeated either the external, or the internal enemy. For victory, a politico-military organisation must be established to provide the machinery for a qualitative conversion of revolutionary action in Africa.

B. POLITICO-MILITARY ORGANISATION

The following measures should be taken :

1. The formation of the All-African People's Revolu- tionary Party (AAPRP) to co-ordinate policies and to direct action.

2. The creation of an All-African People's Revolutionary Army

(AAPRA) to unify our liberation forces and to carry the armed struggle through to final victory.

AAPRP and the All-African Committee for Political Co-ordination (AACPC).

The formation of a political party linking all liberated territories and struggling parties under a common ideology will smooth the way for eventual continental unity, and will at the same time greatly assist the prosecution of the All- African people's war. To assist the process of its formation, an All-African Committee for Political Co-ordination (AACPC) should be established to act as a liaison between all parties which recognise the urgent necessity of conducting an organised and unified struggle against colonialism and neo-colonialism. This Committee would be created at the level of the central committees of the ruling parties and struggling parties, and would constitute their integrated political consciousness.

The AACPC as the political arm of AAPRA would fulfil the following functions :

1. Ensure co-operation between the ruling parties of the liberated territories building socialism, and enable them to support each other in the fight against the internal enemy.

2. Promote widespread and collective ideological training for the cadres of parties teaching the theory of anti-colonialist and anti-neo-colonialist struggle, the case for African unity and for the building of socialism. This would be done in AACPC schools or in political training camps throughout the liberated territories.

3. Co-ordinate and harmonise all political effort and assistance given to the

revolutionary movements in colonised or apartheid areas, and to the progressive forces in all the neo-colonised areas.

4. Provide an organic link with the peoples of Africa, Asia and Latin America who are struggling against imperialism (Organisation of Solidarity with the Peoples of Africa, Asia and Latin America (OSPAAL) .)

5. Ensure permanent relations with the socialist states of the world.

6. Maintain and create links with all workers' move- ments in the capitalist-imperialist states.

Thus the AACPC would emerge as the organisational instrument of a united struggle, and a centralising and disciplinary organ providing permanent contact with the masses and with the scattered centres of their revolutionary activi- ties. Such co-ordination would unify revolutionary action of the vanguard African territories and would enable them to exert decisive influence on the revolutionary liberation movement by allowing them to participate actively in it.

The All-African People's Revolutionary Army (AAPRA)

Members of AAPRA will be the armed representatives of the African people's socialist parties struggling against colonialism and neo-colonialism. They will be the direct product of the African revolutionary, liberation movement, and will be organised as in Chart 5 (Page 64).

These revolutionary armed forces will be under the direction of a high command made up of the military leaders (AAPRA) of the various revolutionary movements in Africa. This in its turn will come under the All-African Committee for Political Co-ordination (AACPC) which represents the political leadership of the entire revolutionary movement. Thus the military, i.e. the armed forces, will always be subordinate to, and under the control of, the political lead- ership.

AAPRA headquarters

The headquarters of the high command of AAPRA will be located in a liberated territory where :

1. The people's power is firmly entrenched.

2. Economic development is advanced enough to enable the territory to provide maximum resistance against imperialist aggression in whatever form it might occur.

3. There are adequate communications, hospitals, printing presses and other essential facilities.

The territory must be in a condition of permanent preparedness for war, all its material and human resources being mobilised to make the area impregnable.

As far as the mobilisation of the people is concerned, trained and armed workers should be organised into mili- tias. Likewise in the agricultural sector, modern agricultural production should be organised along strategic lines. Co- operatives and state farms and other farmers' organisations will constitute the nuclei of self-defence throughout the terri- tory and will be located strategically. Miners, industrial workers, transport employees and others, will be organised into disciplined, self-defence units and will receive military training. Membership of militias will be voluntary and selective.

The militant front thus created will struggle :
- a) For a rapid transformation of the old order
- b) Against internal and external enemies
- c) For the building of socialism.

The struggle will entail hardship and suffering, but it is a phase through which we must pass if we are to accelerate the achievement of a radical, qualitative transformation of the liberation movement. Such measures will result in :

I. the reinforcement of political rectitude and moral strength

II. the abolition of apathy and inertia

III. the achievement of a higher capacity of resistance throughout the population

IV. an improvement of discipline in work and consequently an increase in productivity.

Thus in base areas, it is essential to use the armed forces in conjunction with the masses in order to defeat the enemy. This can best be done through the creation of people's self- defence units (militia) trained to form a broad, united front against imperialism ready to operate anywhere in Africa.

If armed militia are not organised the masses cannot manifest their power in the struggle against the enemy.

In general, a comparatively large territory will provide the best conditions for AAPRA headquarters if it contains a variety of physical features such as mountains, rivers, lakes, forests, plains and even deserts giving partisan de- tachments room to manoeuvre. Usually, the best base areas are in the mountains or near rivers, lakes and estuaries. Those in the plains are generally of a more temporary nature.

AAPRA regional operational commands will be located in appropriate regions of the contested zones.

The AACPC and our revolutionary strategy

The High Command of AAPRA will work in close co- ordination with AACPC, and the smoothness of the liasion will be ensured by the fact that the leaders of the revolutionary movements animating the high command will also be members of AACPC. The programme and the strategy of the revolutionary forces will therefore be drawn up at High Command—AACPC level, on the basis of surveys of the political, economic and military situation in the contested zones and in the enemy-held territories of the continent. Special account will be taken of the objective conditions favouring the liquidation of the oppressive regime in a particular zone or territory.

A study will be made of the pro-revolutionary forces in- side the society under investigation, and an assessment made of the socio-political importance of the workers, peasants and members of the co-operative movement. This assess- ment will be based on the position occupied by the workers in the socio-economic context, the level of their class con- sciousness, and their degree of organisation. In other words, the quality of the group will be a more important criterion than its numerical size.

Investigation along these lines is vital because in order to win a revolutionary war, a prolonged campaign for the support of a crucial social group must be carried out. Like- wise, no socio-economic programme for the winning over of social groups can be drawn up without a clear under- standing of the healthy and strategic elements of the country to be liberated.

Based on attentive study and investigation our revolu- tionary strategy will take into account and exploit the most determinant factors :

A. The existence in Africa of five, broadly differentiated zones :
    a) North
    b) West
    c) South
    d) Central
    e) East

These zones differ widely in climate, natural resources, industrial potential, and in the general pattern of their social and political development.

B. The existence within one zone of varying levels of productive development and of political maturity. For ex- ample, note the difference between conditions in the Republic of South Africa and in South-West Africa, although they are geographically neighbours and are both under enemy control. There is a gap between the productive forces of the Mali—Niger—Dahomey—Togo zone and those of territories like Ghana and Nigeria; but at the same time, the level of political awareness is almost identical amongst the people of Mali, Niger, Ghana, Nigeria and Cameroun.

C. The existence, on the continent, and even inside one zone, of industrial "patches" and of powerful portuary complexes. These represent highly strategic targets for our struggle, and this is why, in certain areas, more attention should be paid to mobilising the proletariat while in other parts attention should first be paid to the rural workers. For example the socio-political lever in one province of a state may be different from the one in another although the same revolutionary struggle is being waged throughout the country as a whole.

Our revolutionary strategy will, therefore be adapted suitably to the variations between zones and territories endowed with important patches of industrialisation, and areas where feudal and patriarchal rural institutions pre-dominate. Again, it will distinguish between territories with a vertical class structure, denoting low development of pro- ductive forces but with an embryo of industrialisation, and territories with a strong modern proletariat force, part of which may be working outside the African continent. The latter may, if organised cohesively, play an important part in the liberation movement by means of sabotage and sub- version at the very core of the capitalist-imperialist states. The study in depth of the objective situation, and the elaboration of a revolutionary strategy are tasks to be under- taken jointly by AAPRA and the AACPC in order to ascertain our own situation at all levels, as well as that of the enemy. The deepening of our knowledge will enable us to avoid wasting our energy in useless skirmishes and battles.

Once the strategic targets and the points of maximum anti-imperialist resistance are determined, the revolutionary forces will know exactly which parts to avoid for the time being, and which to attack first.

There will be no question of AAPRA violating "sover- eignty" when entering a national territory for the purpose of liberating and uniting Africa, since **all** African territory belongs to the African people as a whole, and the will of the African people is expressed in the African revolution.

The army corps

On the basis of our revolutionary strategy the liberation forces of AAPRA will be divided into five armies :

Northern
Western
Southern
Central
Eastern

The divisions constituting the various army corps will be formed from the following sources :

1. Troops allocated to AAPRA by the ruling parties in the liberated territories.

2. Volunteers.

3. Freedom fighter units already in existence.

The creation of our continental people's militia is the logical consequence of the unfolding of the African libera- tion struggle, and it is the essential condition for the emergence of a people's free and united Africa.

CHART 5

AAPRA - AACPC ORGANISATIONAL CHART

A A C P C

AAPRA

Ⓒ Ⓑ Ⓐ

Military Executive
Coordination — Coordination
Army General Staff — Political Executive

Zonal Partisan Command
Coordination — Coordination
Zonal Operational Staff — Zonal Group

Army Staff

North
East
West
Centre
South

Divisional Staff

Coordination
Territorial Partisan Command
Coordination
Territorial Committee

- - - FRONT LINE - - -

Guerrilla Brigade   Guerrilla Brigade

Guerrilla Battalion   Regional Committee

Company   District Committee

Platoon   Village Committee

**LIBERATION MOVEMENT: POLITICAL & MILITARY
(TRIPLE CHAIN OF COMMAND)**

AAPRA's structure and strategy

Since the objectives of the armed liberation forces are both political and military, AAPRA's structure is devised accordingly, with separate chains of command and machinery for co-ordination (Chart 5).

AAPRA divisions C may be used to follow up and com- plete the political and insurrectionary work developed by :

I. the political committees which prefigure the new form of administration to be established in the newly- liberated zone.

II. the guerrilla units

Therefore, AAPRA forces C will act in support of the armed people's struggle and not precede it, although in certain extreme cases, specialised sections of AAPRA can serve as generators of the people's armed struggle by supplying equipment and cadres to the partisan units still lacking such material.

As the people's revolutionary struggle advances, profes- sional armies as such will gradually disappear, until with the achievement of total African liberation and unity, and the establishment of an All-African Union Government they will vanish completely. The defence of Africa will then rest entirely on the continental people's militia.

During the preliminary stag' of the liberation of a particular territory, AAPRA divisions will be stationed in a base area in a nearby liberated zone. However, once the people's struggle has begun inside the contested zone the supporting divisions of AAPRA will camp along the borders of the contested zone. This movement is to be co-ordinated at the level of the regional or zonal army staff and the regional or zonal partisan command, in order to begin the campaign in co-ordination with the territorial partisan command con- cerned. This step is to be decided upon at the level of the Army and Divisional Staff. The result is a vice-like move- ment closing in on the enemy in the contested zone, with the guerrilla units and political committees always ahead of the visible front line. (Chart 6).

Equipment and composition of the armed forces

AAPRA will be a force ready to operate in any part of Africa. It must therefore be equipped with the most modern aircraft, vehicles and weapons, emphasis being placed on firing power, speed, mobility and lightness.

AAPRA will also include specialised, technical units. For example :

Mass psychology teams and units spreading audio- visual and written propaganda by means of radio, films, news-sheets etc.

a) Social service specialists trained to conduct literacy campaigns, to promote child care, public hygiene and other social welfare services

b) technicians specialising in agriculture and in rural processing industries

c) cattle raising and fishery specialists

d) medical officers

e) cultural experts.

Members of AAPRA are not to be considered primarily as professional soldiers, but as

civilians trained in arms, highly qualified fighters who are at the same time efficient workers. They will act to serve, not to subjugate, the broad masses.

Our war is not a war of conquest, it is a war of revolutionary liberation. We fight not only in self-defence but to
free, unite and reconstruct.

STRATEGIC PLAN

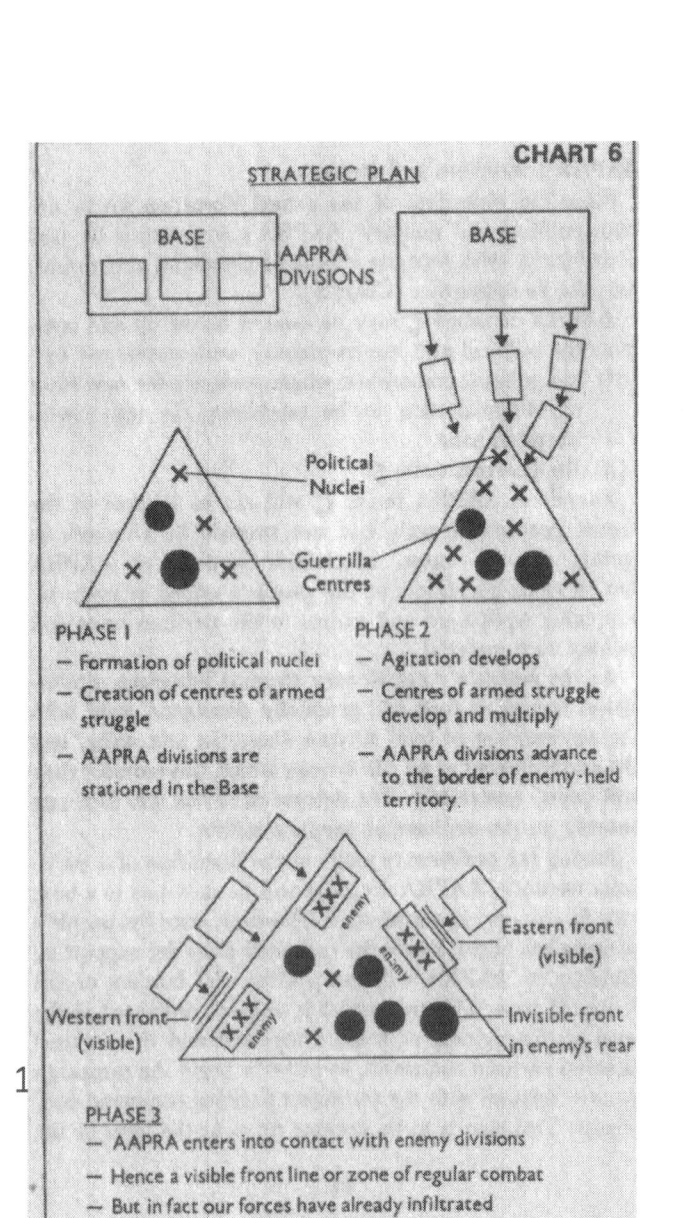

CHART 6

BASE — AAPRA DIVISIONS

BASE

Political Nuclei

Guerrilla Centres

PHASE 1
- Formation of political nuclei
- Creation of centres of armed struggle
- AAPRA divisions are stationed in the Base

PHASE 2
- Agitation develops
- Centres of armed struggle develop and multiply
- AAPRA divisions advance to the border of enemy-held territory.

Western front (visible)

Eastern front (visible)

Invisible front in enemy's rear

PHASE 3
- AAPRA enters into contact with enemy divisions
- Hence a visible front line or zone of regular combat
- But in fact our forces have already infiltrated the territory and the invisible front is in the enemy's rear

Recruitment

It is from the broad masses of the people that the revolutionary liberation movement is born, and it is therefore from among the peasants, workers, members of co-operatives and youth that AAPRA will draw its main strength. In recruiting volunteers, preference will initially be given to members of organisations of an All-African character:

   a) peasants' organisations
   b) trade unions
   c) progressive students' organisations
   d) youth organisations
   e) women's organisations
   f) co-operative movements.

These forces will be supplemented by volunteers allocated to AAPRA by progressive and militant African

CHART 7

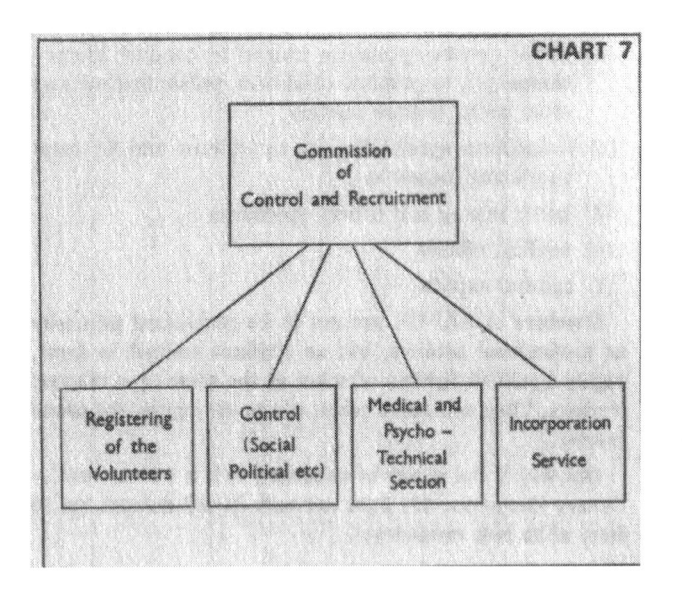

Commission of Control and Recruitment

- Registering of the Volunteers
- Control (Social Political etc)
- Medical and Psycho-Technical Section
- Incorporation Service

parties and governments. (Chart 7).
Before enrolling a volunteer, the Commission of Control and Recruitment will investigate :

1. his social origin
2. his qualities as a worker and as a man
3. his ideological orientation.

He will then undergo tests to assess his character, intellectual capacity, moral fibre and physical fitness.

Enemy agents and adventurers of all kinds will attempt to join AAPRA. We must be constantly on the alert to recognise them and prevent them from infiltrating our revolutionary armed forces. For this reason, particular attention will be paid to tests designed to discover if the volunteer is ideologically sound, and if he has given a true account of his origin and previous place of employment.

As the armed liberation struggle develops and expands, whole units of African troops at present being used by the enemy (on their principle of "let African fight African"), will desert and want to join the AAPRA forces. These troops will be welcomed and given every encouragement. But as soon as possible they will be "screened" individually in accordance with regular AAPRA procedure, and will receive ideological instruction.

General principles of training

Since members of the revolutionary armed forces have social, political and military responsibilities, recruits will go through various levels of training in these three spheres. The aim of our training is not to turn our men into killing machines or mercenaries, but into mature and progressive men intellectually and materially equipped for their revolu- tionary tasks.

The quality and training of recruits for revolutionary units is of particular importance:

a) because our effective strength will, at the start, be much lower than the enemy's numerical strength, (often as low as ten to one).
b) because by the very nature of his performance, and because our initial effective force is comparatively small, the African revolutionary fighter must be a highly specialised soldier.

Thus, the initial military imbalance between ourselves and the enemy will be compensated for by our technical and moral superiority.

All recruits will receive the same basic training, and will then proceed to specialist courses to prepare them for the specialised units of AAPRA.

Commanders of revolutionary armed units will constantly bear in mind the need to

carry out frequent checks on all members of AAPRA :
 a) to make sure that the highest standard of work and
performance of duty is maintained
b) to test morale (the will to fight).

They will also see that organisational machinery is tightly consolidated, and that ideological training is thoroughly and regularly pursued.

It is not the object of our education and training to turn out men who are servilely obedient, but men who respect discipline and are efficient and active because they are fully committed to the revolutionary struggle.

Instead of promoting hierarchic, coercive and follow-like- sheep relationships, our training will seek to develop an intelligent, egalitarian, critical and self-critical outlook within the armed forces. Our fighters will be self-disciplined, revolutionary men and women.

Training courses (social-political-military) will be given training centres located in a base area in an already con- solidated, liberated zone. It is necessary to have several centres operating in different territories or regions. Such centres must remain secret.

Before the volunteers are sent to the centres they will be put under observation in schools where they will receive
basic education and political instruction, and pursue courses
designed to develop their faculties of observation and deduction.

During this stage, the final process of screening and recruiting will be applied, and the unsuitable volunteers rejected.

At the end of the basic course, the successful recruits will be directed to primary training centres. Physical training

The body and its physical endurance must be weathered, strengthened and developed by exercise and by exposure to many varied conditions.

For example :

- a) marching under conditions of duress
- b) camping in difficult terrain
- c) subsisting on short rations for limited periods

d) enduring periods of isolation in small groups cut off from base

e) carrying out rigorous individual initiative and endurance tests.

Daily exercises will help to promote both physical and moral stamina.

Our troops must be trained to operate equally effectively face to face with the enemy, and in various guises, behind
the enemy lines. They should be taught the art of impersonation,
and how to conduct themselves if captured and interrogated.

The development of speed and skill is of the greatest importance in practicing:

I. attacks
II. dispersion

III. regrouping
IV. encircling
V. retreating
VI. close combat
VII. commando-type manoeuvres
VIII. sabotage

Technical training

The aim of the primary training centres is not to form a military élite, but to help our men to establish contact with the concrete realities of the struggle, and to maintain this contact.

The centres will therefore be self-sufficient, and the men will engage in farming, plantation work and cattle-raising on adjacent plots of land as part of their daily tasks. They will be taught to set up small handicraft and processing industries to manufacture uniforms and equipment, (shoes, cartridge belts, ammunition, light arms, etc.) This will enable the AAPRA budget to concentrate on the purchase of military and transport equipment which cannot be manu- factured locally, while leaving the major part of provis- ioning and clothing to the men themselves.

Military training

The practice of shooting will be given special emphasis, for "marksmanship is the core of apprenticeship." In this field, the guerrilla-fighter must be very skilled for it is necessary to use a minimum of ammunition.

Recruits will be taught to use a varied range of arms, and to shoot with deadly accuracy at fixed and moving
targets.

The use of explosives will also be taught. Apart from acquiring a thorough knowledge of all kinds of AAPRA
arms and equipment, pupils of the training centres must:

- a) study and be familiar with equipment used by the
- b) enemy

- c) recognise the different types of aircraft the enemy uses or is likely to use in the various regions of our national territory

- d) learn to make full use of any supplies captured from the enemy.

Political education Every fighter must know :

1. Against whom he is fighting

2. Why he is fighting.

Political education should centre on the key motive for the war—the will to be free. Our essential objective is to
build a socialist society promoting better living and working conditions for all—a socialist society under a Union Government of Africa.

Each recruit will, during the course of his training, attend classes in which the ideological aspects of our
struggle will be explained and discussed.

He will study such subjects as, for example:

    (i) African history

    (ii) Pan-Africanism

    (iii) Socialism tin Africa and in the world context)

    (iv) Imperialism and neo-colonialism.

Teachers will encourage recruits to express their own views, and to discuss any current political, social, economic,
or religious problems which may interest them. Discussions between recruits from different parts of Africa will be particularly valuable in stimulating mutual understanding and dedication to the common ideal of continental liberation and unity.

Leadership

The egalitarian nature of AAPRA forces should eliminate or reduce to a minimum the hierarchic partitioning of ranks. Instead, our forces will be characterised by a well-planned division of revolutionary labour between intelli- gent and purposeful men. Intimidation and bossing must be relentlessly fought against because it is based on a hierarchic, pyramid-like conception of authority which is merely a useful screen for the rise to power of ambitious and petty- minded men.

However, it is vital that certain men should assume command, and in this connection useful reference may be made to the solution provided by the Cuban revolution where ranks are only introduced from lieutenancy upwards, and revolutionary fighters pass directly from the rank of ordinary soldier to that of lieutenant, but only as a result of acts of initiative and courage shown in the course of the struggle.

Our revolutionary fighters must be so highly-trained and self-reliant that each one of them is capable of assuming responsibility if the need arises.

Authority and subordination are required in the organisation of any collective effort, and this applies particularly in military affairs where discipline is essential. But the idealisation of leaders must be guarded against. The general must be **seen not in isolation from the masses,** but as **inseparable from them.**

No general, however skilled, can be successful without the loyal support of inspired, disciplined men who have a thorough knowledge of the issues at stake in the war, are
prepared to make any sacrifice required of them, and have
confidence in his leadership.
The people are the makers of history and it is they who,
in the final analysis, win or lose wars.

Thus, the leaders of our armed forces will be the representatives of the political leadership of our great liberation struggle, and will express the basic interest of the entire African nation.

C. OUR HUMAN FORCES
African society cannot be divided into clearcut, sharply differentiated classes because :

> 1. Too many complex and varying factors criss-cross and interact rendering the socio-economic groups fluid and interdependent.
>
> 2. The level of development of the means of production is still too low. Nevertheless, there does exist an emerging pattern of social groups, some of which are more developed than others. Most of them are potentially revolutionary. But in sharp contrast, there is a surface "scum" of puppets, opportunists and local reactionaries. It must be our aim to bring out the revolutionary potentials

of all sections of African society, though our initial campaign must be directed towards peasants and workers
and members of co-operative movements where revolutionary awareness is high.

The structure of AAPRA-AACPC, the politico-military organisation of our united revolutionary front, will be animated by :

a) the peasants

b) the workers in industries, mines and trade

c) the enlightened elements of the petty bourgeoisie, i.e. the revolutionary petty bourgeoisie, some of whom will help to organise and canalise the people's insurgency against imperialist aggression into a real revolutionary struggle.

d) students

e) certain anti-imperialist elements of the local bourgeoisie, i.e. the patriotic bourgeoisie
f) co-operative and farmers' movements
g) nationalist bureaucratic bourgeoisie

h) revolutionary outsiders, i.e. those elements who have dissociated themselves from the conservative ideology connected with their class origin. These are usually young men and women with a certain educational background.

Some of these forces may be temporarily oppressed and weakened; and their level of economic, cultural and educa- tional development may be heterogeneous.

The peasants

Our liberation struggle must be based on the immense, revolutionary potential of the peasantry :

a) Because the peasants form the overwhelming majority of our population
b) Because the revolutionary units live in their midst and depend on their assistance to survive, and on their active participation in order to develop.

The winning over of the peasant sector is in fact, a funda- mental necessity. We must first make a careful investigation of the condition of our peasantry, the traditional patterns and relationships of production, and the basic problems of agricultural development. There is urgent need for:

    a. an improvement of existing farming and irrigation

    b. more widespread use of fertilisers

    c. a co-ordinated programme of pest control

d. greater research facilities

e. technical training.

In short, we are faced with,
I.   an educational problem
II. a problem of capital investment
III. the need to rationalise the use of the existing means of production, and to introduce new methods.

The task of the revolutionary cadres is therefore not primarily to satisfy land hunger but to awaken the peasants to the realities of their economic potential, and to win them over to a new form of organisation of agricultural production and distribution.

These forces are from the bread masses, are in absolute majority, and must be matured, organised, trained and drawn into the struggle against exploitation and poverty throughout the continent.

The rural proletariat

The agricultural labourers who are the quickest to grasp the problems of the revolution and the inevitability of the struggle are mainly those who produce such goods as cotton, sisal, cocoa, coffee, rubber, citrus fruits, etc., in other
words those employed within the orbit of international trade and industry. It is precisely in this sector that our agricultural workers are massively absorbed, and it is these workers who are in daily contact with modern economic
realities and exploitation.

They are the strategic links in the chain of exploitation of our material and human resources which we are determined to break.

The task will not be difficult since agricultural wage- earners (plantation workers, cattle farmers, African farmers working in a family or semi co-operative system of agricultural production) are the easiest to persuade that the ending of exploitation is the prerequisite of :
1. modernisation and accelerated development in agriculture
2. improvement of working conditions for all workers and peasants and that conditions (a) and (b) are the necessary prelude to the industrialisation of our territories, and a full possibility of self-realisation.

Neo-colonialist control over the advanced sectors of production.

It must be remembered, however, that imperialism in its neo-colonialist stage, and particularly in Africa, draws the bulk of its profits from its grip over the advanced sectors of production:
- (a) mining
- (b) manufacturing
- (c) commerce
- (d) retail trade
- (e) transport
- (f) fisheries (either through direct control over open-sea fishing enterprises or through indirect control over the production of ice, indispensable for the conserva- tion of fish).

Enterprises in the above-mentioned sectors attract about 90% of all western capital invested in Africa, and are there- fore the main areas of neo-colonialist expansion. Conversely, imperialism is increasingly withdrawing from the agricultural sector, leaving its exploitation to indigenous elements.

There is nothing magnanimous about the imperialists' with- drawal from this sector : they are simply placing their stakes in the sectors best suited to their own interests. Indeed, although agriculture absorbs the majority of the African working population:

I. the agricultural sector is, in general, not highly productive because modern techniques have not been widely applied
II. the promotion of agricultural production requires heavy capital investment which is recoverable only on a long term basis. For example, irrigation schemes, the construction of training centres, use of fertilisers, purchase of agricultural machinery,

      involve large capital outlay and a high degree of organisation.

III.   the unpopular equation: plantation = settling=colonialism has remained anchored in the minds of too many progressive Africans for neo-colonialists to venture back into agricultural exploitation. No foreigners can now afford to revert to the old pattern of rural slavery used in the time of old-fashioned colonialism.

In certain states, where no revolution took place to make a clean sweep of the settlers, as in Algeria, foreign settlers are either trying to re-orientate their activities into sectors which are less dangerous from a psychological point of view; or are trying to sell their plantations to high-ranking nationals in order to retire abroad with their ill-gotten fortunes. The explosive situation existing in some African countries where the crucial problem of land still under foreign control has remained unsolved in the post-independence period is enough to discourage any enterprise in this direction by new-style colonialists.

The present nature of imperialist objectives shows up clearly in the fact that over two-thirds of the capital injected into Africa by the major capitalist countries (USA, Great Britain, West Germany, France, Italy, Japan) goes to South Africa, Rhodesia and Katanga. This trend is not coincidental, nor is it due to any marked preference for the type of government in power in these territories. Western capital pours into them because they are the wealthiest mineral, industrial and strategic nucleii on our continent. The second important magnetic pole for imperialist interests is northern Sahara, with its oil, gas, manganese and iron. The remainder of western capital is directed towards commercial business and various other projects where the line between orthodox procedure and corruption and subversion, is al- most impossible to draw.

The huge turnover figures of important trading firms (SCOA, UTC, UAC, PZ, etc.) implanted in Africa, are ex- pressed in the soaring graphs published in company reports. The reason here is that the opportune relaxation of the colonial grip has enabled many Africans to quench freely an increasing craving for capitalist, habit-forming consumer goods introduced by colonialism as the status symbols of "civilisation" and "modernity" associated with the prestige of political power.

We may therefore conclude that :

1. It is as correct as ever to base our struggle on the mobilisation of the majority, i.e. the workers and peasantry

2. We must, at the same time, penetrate the very heart of imperialist and neo-

colonialist centres of exploita- tion by winning the workers to our side.

We must have every inch of our land and every one of our mines and industries.

Workers in the mines, industries and trade

The industrial proletariat is indispensable to our struggle because workers in this sector are :

1. The essential labour force for the continued existence of neo-colonialism, i.e. of the continued exploitation of Africa by alien economic interests

The human lever of the economic and social revolu- tion which is the constructive aspect of our war against imperialism.

The importance of winning over the workers in the key sector of our economy and of integrating them as powerful forces in our revolutionary struggle is recognised and accepted by all genuinely progressive Africans. Yet in recent years a certain amount of confusion has been caused by the spread of myths denying the existence of a working class in Africa. Those who spread these myths are generally African political "personalities" often in government circles, who have an opportunist petty bourgeois outlook and a deep-seated fear of the masses. It is not that they are blind to realities, but they deliberately ignore the existence of a social force whose development might lead to the destruction of the very clique from whom they receive income and privilege.

Even before the advent of puppets, the imperialists did all in their power to avoid the emergence of an organised African working class:

a) for a long time, the French prevented the workers in their colonies from forming trade unions
b) the English integrated "TUC advisers" into their colonial administration to set up trade unions tailored to western capitalist standards.

Later, the puppets and their local reactionary partners continued to refuse to recognise the existence of the ex- ploited classes which had emerged in African society, in order to avoid exposing the class of exploiters of which they themselves were the leaders.

They refuse to see the workers because they believe they can thus prevent the workers from seeing them and tearing them to pieces. But not even a so-called "élite" can bury its head in the sand for very long.

Consequently, African reactionaries were soon compelled to make certain concessions to reality to avoid being en- gulfed by the rising tide of discontent. They resorted to the well-known ritual of setting up puppet trade unions to stifle the workers' movement by creating

1. employers' trade unions
2. clerks' trade unions controlled by a swarm of white- collared employees who are not directly involved in the productive process, and who poison the workers' movement
3. unions dominated by corrupted leaders.

The high degree of attention paid to the workers by neo- colonialists indicates their crucial importance in the revolutionary struggle. They are paid comparatively high wages, and led to believe that if the imperialists withdraw they will be unemployed. In some cases, they are given houses at reduced rents and "amenities" to keep them happy while they are being exploited, and to lull them into a false sense of security and well-being. The object of this attention is to instil into them the idea that they have something to gain by a continuance of the imperialist way of life, and everything to lose by a revolution.

This kind of indoctrination makes the task of drawing the workers into the ranks of our liberation struggle some- what difficult. But then nothing is easy in a revolutionary situation, and already, hundreds of thousands of African workers are aware of their true position and are ready to act.

Neo-colonialist attempts at integration

Probably the most insidious of the enemy's attempts to win the African workers to their side is the campaign to "integrate" them into the neo-colonialist, capitalist system of exploitation. This is the so-called solution of "Africanisation", made palatable by the promise of wages and salaries equal to those of foreign workers.

The main problem for our workers is not that an African earns three, five or ten times less than his western counter-part, but that he, like they, is exploited, and will never be able to achieve full self-realisation within the imperialist, capitalist system.

Far from constituting a serious challenge to the system, Africanisation harmonises and attempts to rationalise it so that its running is more smooth and efficient, and there- fore more profitable for the enemy.

The truth behind the salaries

In South Africa, where African workers live in conditions close to slavery, the fascist-racist regime is obliged to give its mining and industrial workers comparatively better salaries than those usually paid in the rest of Africa for a similar job. However, this fact does not prove that workers have something to gain from the apartheid regime, or that they occupy a ̄ privileged" position in relation to the rest of the African workers. On the contrary, such salary scales are a clear indication that the enemy cannot do without this labour force, and this is true both in the colonised and neo- colonised territories in Africa. For example, if all African miners in South Africa withdrew their labour the country's economy would be paralysed and political power within their grasp. Such is the potential and, as yet, unrealized strength of our workers.

At present, it might appear that African workers are only ready to strike for increases in salary. If this is the case, it can only mean one of two things :

1. That they are unable to attempt any other form of action in the conditions prevailing at their places of work
2. Or that they are not yet aware that there is something else to be done.

The first alternative is due to measures taken by the enemy. The second, is the result of both enemy measures and revolutionary deficiencies :

a) The enemy both needs and fears the African labour force, and therefore does its utmost to arrest the in- tellectual and professional development of the workers by keeping them in the unskilled category for life.
b) African revolutionaries have not yet been successful in explaining to the workers the crucial part they can play in the liberation struggle.

In certain extreme cases, the purely economic form of struggle has definite positive aspects. But it is becoming increasingly true that in Africa, particularly in the zones of intensive mining and industrial activity, this form of struggle can only achieve very limited results, and does not match up to the urgency of the situation.

Being forced to abandon working-sites so strategically and economically indispensable to the enemy cannot be a solution for the workers. But the presence of African workers inside neo-colonialist strongholds opens up interesting possibilities for a quick and thorough liquidation of the enemy.

It is essential for the leaders of the revolutionary libera- tion movement :
 1. To bring the truth out into the open 2. To establish close and active contact with the African

workers

3. To link the African workers' movement organically
to the struggle by determining specific intermediary
objectives so that whatever progress is achieved in the workers' struggle will mean progress in the whole
anti-imperialist movement, and the promotion of socialism on a continental scale.

The failure of imperialist tactics to prevent the workers from realising their true
position, and to avoid the immense strength of the African workers
from being unleashed inside the strongholds of neo-colonialism,
the enemy does its utmost to disintegrate the workers' movement, rendering it spineless and isolating the workers
from the realities of African society, and above all from the revolutionary movement,

during the whole of the time they spend on the working-sites.

However, the enemy can never manage to cut them off completely, for one of the essential features of African
labour is its mobility. The workers' movement and revolutionary strategy
Even in territories under intense enemy control no worker in the modern economic sector :
I. is totally isolated from the broad masses
II. or permanently established on his working-site under enemy surveillance.

Inside enemy strongholds and in key positions, African workers remain part of a vast mobile force. They come from the reserves, villages, rural areas and neighbouring territories to work for a stipulated period of time in the factories, mines, plantations, harbours or transport centres.

Once the contract is terminated they return to their homes either permanently, or to stay for a while before once again setting out to obtain work.

The permanent mobility of the African labour force was encouraged, and even deliberately organised in places, by the enemy, in order to avoid confrontation with a corporate and fully-constituted African proletariat. But this very mobility has proved of great value to the revolutionary movement. Mobile workers establish an active liaison be- tween the rural population and the centres of neo-colonialist strength. They penetrate the innermost strongholds of the enemy and are becoming qualified to take them over.

Therefore, if our revolutionaries are faced with major difficulties in their attempts to educate and organise the workers on the working-sites, they must seek their :

1. original points of departure
2. transit points.

It is at the points of departure, and along the lines of transit that political education must be specialized. Once the workers' trajectories have been determined, mobile teams specialized in propaganda work and in political agitation, may even infiltrate into the circuit, enabling revolutionaries and revolutionary ideas to penetrate the very bloodstream of the enemy's economy. (Chart 8).

Therefore, the integration of the workers in the revolutionary struggle may be achieved through various means and at different levels,—methods and arguments varying according to conditions and circumstances. Any action taken by workers to advance their position is an integral part of our revolutionary struggle. For example :

a) in an enterprise under foreign capitalist control, when- ever the workers claim a rise in pay

b) in an enterprise under indigenous capitalist control,

CHART 8

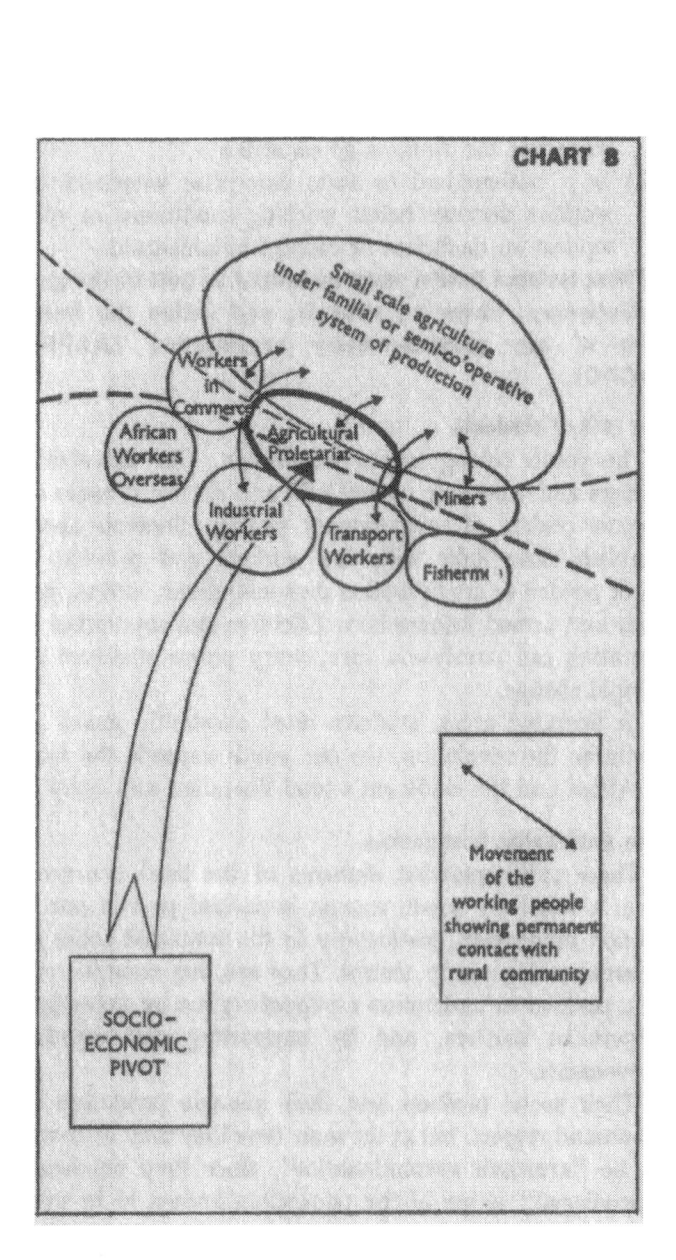

Small scale agriculture under familial or semi-co'operative system of production

Workers in Commerce

African Workers Overseas

Agricultural Proletariat

Industrial Workers

Transport Workers

Miners

Fishermen

Movement of the working people showing permanent contact with rural community

SOCIO-ECONOMIC PIVOT

whenever the workers go on strike

(iii) in a nationalised or state enterprise whenever the workers demand better working conditions, or rebel against an inefficient or corrupt administrator.

These isolated battles must be fought as part of the great revolutionary, liberation struggle, and within the frame- work of our politico-military organisation (AAPRA- AACPC).

The role of students

The youth belong to the Revolution. Our universities, colleges and schools in enemy-held and contested zones can become centres of revolutionary protest. Students should establish close links with the workers and provide the spark needed to set in motion demonstrations, strikes, boy- cotts and armed insurrection. Effective student-worker co- operation can paralyse a reactionary power structure and compel change.

In liberated areas, students must constantly guard and revitalise the revolution. On our youth depends the future of Africa and the continent's total liberation and unity.

The nationalist bourgeoisie

These anti-imperialist elements of the local bourgeoisie form a relatively small, though important part of our lib- eration movement, particularly in the contested zones and in areas under enemy control. They are, for example, often in a position to undermine a puppet regime by exposing its imperialist masters, and by supporting anti-imperialist movements.

Their social position and their genuine patriotism will command respect, but at the same time they may be thought to be "armchair revolutionaries", since they represent a "privileged" sector of the population known to be out of sympathy with our socialist objectives. This should not dis- courage our revolutionary cadres from drawing them into the main stream of our movement since they can be of inestimable help in achieving our first two objectives of liberation and continental unity, and many of them may, in the course of the struggle become convinced of the need for socialism.

Revolutionary outsiders

These include :

1. Africans who have dissociated themselves from the ideology connected with their class origin

2. Men and women of African descent living overseas
3. Foreigners who for various reasons have become interested in the African revolution, and wish to take an active part in the revolutionary struggle.

There is room for all these people in our great struggle. For our objective remains the same throughout, to mobilise all the human forces at our disposal in order to create a decisive, revolutionary, flexible and multiform *striking force.*

The role of women

The women of Africa have already shown themselves to be of paramount importance in the revolutionary struggle. They gave active support to the independence movement in their various countries, and in some cases their coura- geous participation in demonstrations and other forms of political action had a decisive effect on the outcome. They have, therefore, a good revolutionary record, and are a great source of power for our politico-military organisation. Maximum use must be made of their special skills and potentialities.

First, it is necessary to examine the nature of the African woman's resources in terms of the revolutionary struggle, and then to determine how these can best be used and developed.

The following is a proposed questionnaire of some essential points to be studied by our revolutionary cadres, concerning the position of women in African society.

I. In statistical and qualitative terms, how has the African woman assimilated the two-fold experience of our traditional, communalistic society? That is, how does she stand in relation to the Euro-Christian experience of colonialism and neo-colonialism, and to the Islamic experience?

II. What is the nature of her links and/or dependence on the imperialist oppressor? How can these links be used to the advantage of our revolution?

III. Sometimes these links are predominantly economic, for example in the relationship between the super-mammies and the foreign trading firms. In other cases, the links may be purely personal. Prostitution in the colonial and neo-colonial context combines personal and economic dependence on the monied class, with political links in the form of espionage and collaboration.

IV. To what extent is the African woman's revolutionary role a prolongation, a modification, or a total departure from her traditional communalistic milieu and her duties, rights and general position? How does it affect her subjective views of emancipation and happiness?

V. To what extent did she formerly take part in produc- tive work?

VI. Is she entitled to the fruits of her labour? In what proportion

VII. How far is the practice of polygamy synonymous with feudalism? And to what extent does this practice mean that the African woman is exploited?

VIII. In which specific cases can it be said that women in Africa are exposed to a two-fold exploitation as workers (i.e. class exploitation in the Marxist sense of the term), and as *women?*

In the case of each social-ethnic group under analysis, the final ratio of the positive answers to the negative ones will determine the nature of the efforts to be made to ful- fil the final objective which is the same throughout Africa : the revolutionary mobilisation of African women.

Women in enemy-held zones

Women in zones under enemy control must participate fully in the work of political education and organisation.

The influence of women over the youth of the country, and the fact that they are the wives, sisters, and mothers of future freedom fighters must be utilised to the full by the revolutionary cadres.

The degree of a country's revolutionary awareness, may be measured by the political maturity of its women.

They are in a particularly strong position to infiltrate the enemy ranks since they can exploit the lack of austerity, the mercenary state of mind, and the feeble sense of purpose which are characteristic of the counter-revolutionary soldier.

Women in the bases and liberated areas

The majority of women in these areas, particularly mothers and older women, can ensure the continuity of the consolidation process and the growth of self-sufficiency and preparedness, while the men within the action units remain essentially in preparedness for war.

Their main tasks, inside the liberated zones where creative work can begin, is to ensure self-sufficiency, stability and resistance on all levels.

The training of women

If they satisfy the physical, social and ideological recruitment standards determined by the Commission of Control and Recruitment of AAPRA, women may join the training centres on the same basis as men, and be eligible for the same responsibilities and authority. They will receive similar political, military and social training as men, the courses being adapted to their capacities and physical strength.

Comparatively more emphasis will be placed on:

a. Political instruction

1. Propaganda techniques. The following tasks can be usefully fulfilled by women in the bases:

   i. the production and reproduction of leaflets

   ii. the distribution and explanation of newspapers, news-sheets, slogans and instructions to the local population.

   iii. dramatisation of repressive incidents; the organization of victim's funerals with a political dimension; demonstrations of passive resistance; the production of placards, banners and other insignia.

Intelligence work. For example, women "petty" traders and "market" women can use the mobility required by their trade as a cover for the carrying of messages, arms and intelligence reports.

3. Interpreting and liaison duties. Women who can speak more than one language will be invaluable as interpreters, and for the interrogation of prisoners.

4. Administrative, judicial and secretarial activities. For example, women should be trained to replace men in local government.

Reliable and efficient secretaries will be needed to ensure the smooth running of the AAPRA-AACPC organisation, to keep records and to carry out other essential office work.

b. Education

A nursery and primary school should be attached to each
production unit, workshop or medical centre organised by women. These will absorb :

    a. the children of the women workers

    b. AAPRA orphans and freedom fighters'

c. children of the local population

Trained infant and primary school teachers will be assisted by working mothers taking turns to help in the general duties of caring for the children.

Likewise, each production unit should elect its literacy campaigning group to persuade adults to study after working
hours. Incentives may be usefully employed; and a moderate degree of competitiveness between the various groups will also help to encourage maximum effort.

The close network of secondary schools, which it should be the ultimate goal of every liberated zone to possess. should be utilised for evening lectures and class discussions.

c. Medical training

Hospitals, first aid posts, infant and child welfare centres, and birth control clinics will be set up in the base areas, and will be staffed largely by women.

Nurses with suitable guerrilla training will be attached as regulars to the action units.

d. Driving instruction

We cannot afford to waste a single fighting man on non- combat duties. Women should, therefore, be trained to drive the many different vehicles used within the AAPRA- AACPC organisation, cars, lorries, jeeps and so on.

e. The provisioning of AAPRA forces

1. Food. In view of the increasing involvement of men in part-time or full-time guerrilla activities, the responsibility of producing and distributing sufficient food for all will belong mainly to the women. In areas not yet liberated, freedom fighters

in action units will encourage the local women to take over food produc- tion duties from the men, so that more local men can be recruited into the permanent guerrilla force. Farming, fishing, food stocking and preservation will be increasingly done by women.

Interest in food preservation techniques, and time-saving methods involving minimum expense should be encouraged. Dependence on provisions from external allies should be lessened to promote local qualities of autarchy.

The local population as a whole is the main pro-vider of food, but since it is the primary objective of guerrilla activities to absorb increasing numbers of local men into the action units, the women will remain as the only permanent, full-time producers and distributors of food.

Women in the bases and liberated areas will set up permanent or mobile distribution centres, canteens and people's shops. They will supervise the rationing of scarce commodities, and organise barter activities in regions where the use of the enemy's currency is barred.

2. Clothing. Women will be trained to set up and operate workshops for the manufacture of uniforms, covers, canvas bags, shoes and other equipment needed by the freedom fighters.

D. PROPAGANDA

Propaganda is a means of liberation, an instrument of clarification, information, education and mobilisation.

It serves two different but essential functions in our war :
1. To subvert the enemy
2. To awaken and mobilise our people.

Propaganda to subvert the enemy.

An indispensable preliminary to battle is to attack the mind of the enemy, to undermine the will to fight so that the result of the battle is decided before the fighting begins. The revolutionary army attacks an irresolute and demora- lised army.

This type of propaganda must have two main objectives:
a) to undermine the morale of non-African troops, ex- posing the injustice of their cause and the certainty of their defeat.
b) to encourage African troops who have been misled into fighting for the enemy, to desert and join AAPRA.

The main problem in both cases is the difficulty of access, or communication, particularly in enemy-held zones. Broadcasts, the distribution of leaflets, and the holdings of secret meetings and discussions are some of the methods most likely to produce results.

In contested zones, where revolutionaries operate more freely, all the various media of propaganda can be used, (e.g. radio, television, cinema, press, exhibitions).

Propaganda addressed to the people

The object of this propaganda is to :

    i. denounce enemy action to the people

    ii. explain our cause

iii. mobilise the masses so that they break free from inertia and participate actively in the revolutionary struggle.

This can be done on two levels :

1. Theoretically, by accelerating the political awakening of the majority. Such an awakening often occurs
in phases with the spread of :

   a. the idea of an independent existence (anti-colonialism, nationalism)

   b. the idea that "something is rotten" (the awakening to neo-colonialist exploitation)

   c. the idea that the situation can change (i.e. a conscious anti-neo-colonialist attitude)

d. the idea that victory can be achieved only by action (the need to use force; the will to fight).

2. On a practical level, by integrating our educational work within the politico-military organisation (AAPRA-AACPC), and providing the actual means for carrying out our revolutionary aims.

The suggested mechanism of our revolutionary struggle is illustrated in detail in Chart 5 on page 64.

Chart 9 (page 97) is a simplified plan to show the nature and functions of the triple chain of command.

Structure A, the political executive, is to carry out intensive and extensive political education. This structure branches out to village level in the rural areas, and to wards in the townships. A will gradually provide

the oppressed. exploited and dissatisfied masses with political organization and education. The people will thus become an informed.
organised and determined force.

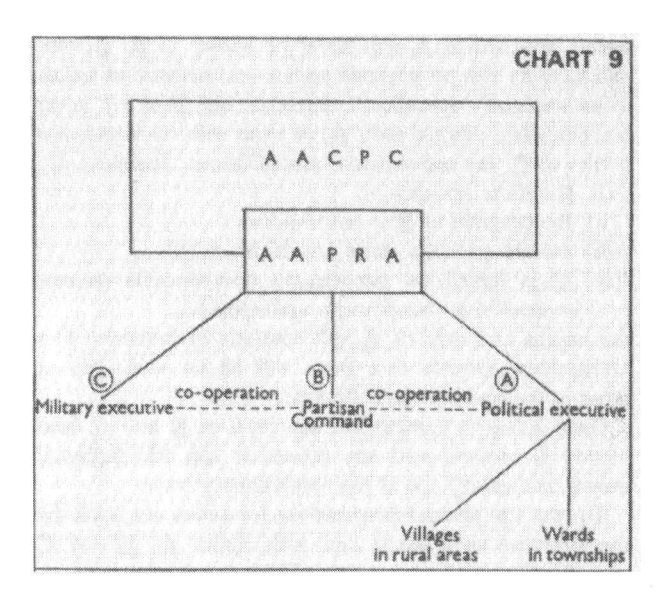

CHART 9

A A C P C

A A P R A

Ⓒ Military executive --- co-operation --- Ⓑ Partisan Command --- co-operation --- Ⓐ Political executive

Villages in rural areas   Wards in townships

B comes into being as a result of the successful work achieved by **A** in co-ordination with the Military Executive which specialises in the practical organisation of the revolutionary units.

When action is initiated, through the joint decision of the Political Executive, the Military Executive and the

Army General Staff, chain **B** assumes foremost importance.
In the meantime **A** pursues its organisational work and even reinforces it, since the action of **B** will often be carried out on the basis of the preliminary work done by **A** or on the strength of information provided by **A.**

A runs a system of propaganda and of intelligence which has certain links with the **B** structure, though it never completely merges with it. In other words, various types of agents attached to **A** will never be known to **B**. **B** itself

will have its own propaganda section and network of agents of an essentially operational character, but these will never be completely merged with **A**, or even with the equivalent
bodies of **C**, the conventional armed forces. Therefore, if :

  i. B suffers reverses

 ii. the progress of B is not uniform

iii. certain guerrilla units are disintegrated

 iv. B is forced by particularly unfavourable circumstances to go temporarily underground, the organs and cells of A will continue to function. This arrangement ensures that there will be no void, gap or lapse in the revolutionary struggle.

Once action is launched at the level of **B** and **C** final victory is assured, and any retreat or loss will represent
only a momentary ebb of the revolutionary wave.

To sum up, general preparations for action are made by the structure as a whole and with chains **A, B** and **C**
co-ordinating with each other. Fieldwork begins with **A**
which creates the conditions for the setting up of B, whose
activity is co-ordinated with **C**.
A, B and **C** constitute a huge, well-equipped ideologically
formed and physically trained force. But the complex
is initially set in motion by propaganda **A**.

The type of propaganda needed is first and foremost organisational and ideological. It is therefore necessary to

have a clear conception of the essential features of the propaganda we need, and a carefully selected and highly
trained corps of agents to spread it.

Our propaganda covers the entire field of revolutionary political education. It is the subjective vector of the
struggle and is based on a chain of constants: clarifying—denouncing—explaining clarifying—denouncing—explaining—**solving** clarifying--solving—**mobilizing**

The chain of propaganda tasks does not vary, but different degrees of emphasis will be laid on one link in the chain rather than on another according to :
I. the level of the audience (national forces or an inter- national public)
II. the specific situation it treats
III. the stage reached in the struggle and the various circumstances conditioning it.

Propagandists will also vary their techniques and themes to suit conditions in the various types of territory they are operating in. For example:
- d) a liberated territory, where the people's power must be consolidated
- e) a contested territory, where the liberation movement must be supported, where popular consensus must be achieved, and where the enemy must be demoralised
- f) an enemy-held territory, where it is essential: to ana- lyse and denounce enemy action; to show the breaks in his armour; to show why and how the people's forces must be organised and led to victory.

Propaganda is spread through various media:
- a) Radio
- b) Television

c) Press (newspapers, pamphlets, leaflets)
d) Cinema (documentaries, news reels)
e) Conferences, discussions, debates
f) Exhibitions (using posters, slides, maps, charts, photographs, documents).

Media a, b, c and d are generally more easily available in liberated zones or bases.

Media c, e and f are adaptable anywhere provided capable cadres and appropriate means are available. The cadres can be trained in AACPC schools.

The ways of producing written propaganda change according to prevailing conditions. In areas where propaganda can be openly produced, printing presses are used.

In a clandestine situation, portable duplicating machines with their compact accessories are suitable.

There are two main kinds of clandestine publications:

1. Leaflets which deal with immediate on-the-spot news, and which spread slogans, rallying-cries and watchwords
2. Bulletins or newspapers.

However, all propaganda media must convey the following ideas, encouragement and information:

  i. the struggle to the death against imperialism and neocolonialism, its agents and all reactionaries

  ii. African liberation and unity, and the construction of a socialist society

iii. news of the problems, progress and achievements of other socialist countries

iv. information about the progress of AAPRA forces

v. practical advice and directions of all kinds for the fighters, workers, peasants, students, women, etc.

Our propagandists must leave no problem untackled, no mistake unexposed. Truth must always be told. It is a proof of strength, and even the hardest truth has a positive aspect which can be used.

Finally, our propaganda must promote self-induced morality, that is, self-reliance, self-education, self-discipline and self-criticism. These qualities are basic in the revolutionary guerrilla fighter who is by nature and training:

a. courageous
b. skillful
c. disciplined
d. loyal.
e.

Our propaganda should undertake to illustrate and demonstrate the necessity of cultivating and consolidating these four qualities, not only subjectively, but scientifically. The revolutionary fighter must by the very nature of his highly specialised performance and the speediness of his action, adopt a scientific attitude in all fields. Superstition, magic or irrational beliefs, fatalism and wishful thinking must be fought against.

Suggestions for propaganda items

a) Blueprint for a monthly AAPRA review
b) Blueprint for a weekly of:

I. the armed forces
II. the military executive
III. the political executive

C. Blueprint of a local revolutionary newspaper or bulletin dealing with various themes:

I. the preliminary phase of the formation of cells
II. the prelude to insurrection
III. the unfolding struggle (victories and reverses expressed in figures, etc.)

D. Blueprint for leaflets:

(i) denouncing the enemy for political and economic reasons
(ii) addressing the various sectors of the population

Since intensive and extensive political education is pioneering work (i.e. preparing the ground for action), and constitutes the

mainstay of action, the political activists in charge of propaganda must be well-grounded in the rules and general principles of action. They must always bear in mind the essential objective, the take-over by the people and workers of:
  I. the civil administration
  II. the police
  III. the armed forces

and control over :
  I. industry
  II. agriculture
  III. mining
  IV. transport

Hence the need for the organisation and mobilisation of the :
  I. workers
  II. peasants
  III. members of co-operatives
  IV. students
  V. youth

VI. women

with specific rules, suggestions and programmes for each sector and in accordance with the supreme objective :

African unity and socialism— To conclude, propaganda must:

a) prepare for the organisation of popular insurrection

b) spread dissension and subversion amongst the enemy's ranks, and undermine morale

c) expose the enemy's propaganda, and attempts to misinform and mislead
d) spread information, intelligence etc.

These basic tasks constitute the necessary prelude to action, the condition for the smooth unfolding of our struggle, and its final guarantee of success,—the achievement of a Union Government of Africa.

**CHAPTER TWO
BASIC PRINCIPLES AND
TECHNIQUES OF
GUERRILLA WARFARE**

The main part of the armed revolutionary struggle will be carried out by centrally-directed guerrilla forces. These will receive expert and rigorous training in base camps where the most modem fighting methods will be taught. The object of the final part of this Handbook is therefore, merely to provide a source of ready reference to some of the fundamental elementary principles and techniques of guerrilla
warfare.

A. ORGANISATION OF A GUERRILLA ARMY

A guerrilla army, although operating in small, widely dispersed groups needs centralised direction and co-ordination.

The following sections must be established :

1. Recruitment
See the section on recruitment for AAPRA forces

2. Information
It is the task of this section to provide information about anything which may have a bearing on the struggle in a particular place.

a) inhabitants : those who are supporters of the revolutionary struggle, those who are enemies, and those who
b) are indifferent physical features of the country : rivers, forests, mountains, valleys, etc.
c) strategical position of towns, roads, bridges, rail- ways, airfields, etc.
d) attitude of members of the armed forces and the police; behaviour of freedom fighters and of those who wish to join them.

The information section is also responsible for :

I. drawing maps

II. espionage and counter-espionage

III. compiling and keeping dossiers on every freedom fighter in the zone

IV. coding and decoding of messages

V. liaison and co-operation with information sections in other zones.

3. Operations

This section must authorise all operations by guerrilla groups. All chiefs of zones must be consulted so that tactics and every aspect of each operation can be discussed. The leader of the guerrilla group which is to carry out the operation will of course take part in the discussions.

4. Sabotage

This is one of the most important sections of guerrilla organisation. The officer in charge must see that the most modern techniques and equipment are employed, that saboteurs are constantly active, and that the enemy's weak points are pin-pointed and attacked and his economic life- lines destroyed.

5. Instruction

The officer commanding this section will be in charge of the training camps for freedom fighters. He will also pro- mote the education of peasants and supervise all other aspects of education in the region.

6. Armament

This section is responsible for the purchase and storage of all fighting equipment, arms and ammunition, and for
its distribution among the guerrilla forces.

7. Provisions

It is the task of the officer in charge of this section to see that revolutionaries are provided with adequate food, uniforms and other supplies.

8. Health

Qualified doctors and nurses will generally be in base camps and hospitals, and may not be able to attend guerrillas who fall sick or who are injured while on operational duties. All members guerrilla groups will receive

first aid instruction in the training camps, and will
carry basic essential medical supplies. The officer in charge of the Health section will ensure that guerrilla groups are adequately equipped medically, and that all sick and wounded brought back to base areas receive prompt medical attention. He will also keep an eye on all health problems
in his area, particularly concerning himself with the prevention of any epidemic spreading to the guerrilla
forces.

9. Propaganda

See Book Two, Chapter One, section D. It is particularly important in guerrilla warfare, where military action is usually unpublicised, that the propaganda section
issues communiques to spread news of revolutionary victories.

This will raise the morale of revolutionary groups,\ and demoralise the enemy.

10. Volunteers

The officer in charge of this section should see that volunteers are given non-combat duties and remain unarmed
until reliable information is obtained about them. The normal recruitment processes of AAPRA will apply to both
men and women volunteers. Where a district or zone has more volunteers than it needs, the central command should
be informed, so that arrangements may be made for volunteers to be transferred to where they are most needed.

11. Communications

Courses in radio telegraphy and in the use of all communications

media will be given in the training camps. It is the task of the communications section, therefore, to organise and supervise the whole communications network of the revolutionary movement, and to see that the latest and best equipment is made available to the guerrilla units.
Guerrilla units

These should normally consist of 10-25 men, though the precise number of men in a unit will depend on fighting conditions and local circumstances. In general, small units are easier to operate, and are often more effective, than larger ones. Members of each unit should be friends, true
brothers who are ready to give their lives in the revolutionary struggle. Numbers of small guerrilla units may form part of a larger guerrilla group under a group commander.

Guerrilla unit and group leaders
Leaders should be:

i. highly-trained, efficient fighters

ii. able to command obedience and to make correct and rapid decisions

iii. patient, and never unjust.

Each guerrilla must know the hierarchy of his unit and group so that when there are casualties, the leadership is never in doubt.

Training

A guerrilla must be :

a. absolutely clear in his mind about what he is fighting for

b. convinced of the justness of his cause

c. a skilled soldier

d. of strong moral fibre

Every guerrilla should be able to :

　i.　shoot with a rifle, revolver and machine gun

　ii.　handle and throw a knife well

　iii.　make and throw bombs

　iv.　march continuously for long periods with very little

　v.　ride a bicycle, paddle a canoe and row a boat

　vi.　climb walls and surmount obstacles with the aid of ropes

　vii.　change and mend wheels on bicycles and cars, and carry out other elementary repairs

　viii.　read and understand maps and know how to make use of them

　ix.　send and receive messages in the morse code.

Not every soldier will be accomplished in all these tasks but the more education and knowledge he has, the greater the chance he has of becoming a good revolutionary fighter.

Equipment

Apart from arms and ammunition, every guerrilla unit should carry certain basic equipment such as first aid supplies, compass, watch, whistles, torches, files, saws,
fishing line and hooks, water bottles, etc. In addition, each guerrilla must always carry a rope of about 2 metres, or some other substitute (e.g. palm tree fibres tied together).

This rope can prevent a comrade from becoming separated from other members of his unit on a dark night, when comrades can tie themselves to each other. It can also be
useful, for example, for crossing rivers, and for securing prisoners.

B. STRATEGY AND TACTICS

The tactics of guerrilla warfare must be subordinate to the strategy of the revolutionary war. Tactics will, therefore, vary according to the particular phases of the struggle, and the activity and actions of the enemy. Attack is the first principle, though there are times when defence is both necessary and useful. These two methods—attack and defence—are therefore closely linked, and basic in guerrilla tactics.

Mobility

According to necessity the guerrilla unit must be able to move in a few minutes from the field of battle, and in a few hours even from the region of struggle.

For this reason it must change its front continually and avoid encirclement—
the most dangerous tactic employed by the enemy.

It is the task of guerrilla units to surprise the enemy, to inflict casualties and destruction, and to disappear without
loss. This is the tactic of surprise attack and rapid disappearance.

Three days is the longest time a guerrilla unit should remain in any one place. On arriving at a new hiding place, tracks and paths must be covered up and no noise made.

Marches should be carried out at night. There should be no talking or smoking. The feet should be lifted high at each step to avoid tripping on stones, branches and other obstacles. During the day, the guerrillas should sleep (in turns), study maps of the region, do special section
work, and so on.

By rapid manoeuvre, guerrilla units are able to :

i. retreat from unfavourable battle conditions, and in this way avoid losses

ii. link up with other guerrilla units to draw the enemy out to cause the greatest material and human damage possible.

Concentration and dispersal of forces

The enemy is numerically superior and better armed **than** the guerrilla army. Guerrilla units must overcome this disadvantage by knowing when to concentrate their forces and when to disperse them. They must concentrate their forces, by linking up with other units and by reinforcements, when the enemy is in a weak position and can be attacked. They must disperse forces when confronted by large confrontations of enemy units, when there is danger of encirclement, and where the terrain is unfavourable.

Bases

A base must be established before a guerrilla move- ment can begin. A village, a section of liberated territory, for example, can serve as a base. It is of vital importance to make the correct choice of site. It must be strategically placed, defensible and secret, and be in an area where the masses solidly support the revolutionary struggle.

Where geographical conditions make the formation of a base impossible, a circle of civil collaborators must be formed .

Choice of objectives for attack

Communications, above all, railways, airfields and roads are some of the most suitable objectives for guerrilla attack. Military transportation, for example, columns of vehicles, troops on the march, convoys of lorries carrying provisions are obvious targets.

The guerrilla unit will occupy positions inaccessible to the enemy, favourable for mobile defence, and which lie in the direction from which the enemy is expected.

The primary condition for the success of an attack is a profound knowledge of the terrain, the exploitation of this knowledge, and careful preparation of the action.

Combat in favourable terrain

In favourable terrain, such as mountains and forests, it is possible to form and train large numbers of guerrillas to construct bases, repair units, dispensaries, education centres, arms depots and so on. Conditions are also favourable for the establishment of contingency forces. With contingency forces, the leader must take into account the terrain, quantity of arms and ammunition at his dis- posal, and the problem of reinforcements.

The sphere of activity of a partisan unit must be as large as conditions permit, and co-ordinate with the activities of neighbouring units. If units mobilise at night, the journey must not be longer than five or six hours from the safe place. Small groups can be sent out of the safe place to reconnoitre, but so as not to alert the enemy, they must not engage in battle before the main force arrives. Where- ever possible, similar arms and ammunition as that used by the enemy should be employed.

Food supplies are difficult to obtain in inaccessible ter- rain. It is necessary, therefore, to form strong liaison with local suppliers to ensure that there is always sufficient. It should be remembered that there are arms and other supplies needed by the guerrilla forces, in enemy supply depots. These depots must be raided and the supplies seized. Guerrilla units must maintain regular liaison with the leaders of the liberation struggle by means of a network of people who are trustworthy, and who will hide pro- visions and emissaries in their houses. Internal liaison must be carried out by radio and various technical means.

Combat in unfavourable terrain

Plains, unforested areas, etc. are, in general, unfavour- able terrain for the operation of guerrilla forces. In these areas, attention must be focussed on the destruction of the enemy's means of communication. It is here that the saboteurs can operate effectively in blowing up bridges, cutting telephone and telegraph wires and so on.

A guerrilla unit in unfavourable terrain should con- sist of from 10 to 15 men, since speed and mobility are vital. For a particular operation, guerrilla units may unite. But they should disperse again immediately after- wards.

Unfavourable terrain usually means dense habitation and farms. This is good country for supplies. Guerrillas must make contact with trustworthy people who will help to supply the unit.

In these circumstances it is not possible to have the amenities of base camps. But guerrillas will be able to depend on support from among the local population. A dense population allows guerrillas to pass information, but at the same time there is greater risk of betrayal. Im- portant messages must be written in code, or sent orally.

Villages

The group of village revolutionaries is responsible for the struggle in their own particular village. The group consists of politically-aware villagers who live side by side with the other inhabitants, but who maintain contact with the guerrilla units operating in the region.

A group of village revolutionaries can be established only when the area borders on a zone occupied by the liberation movement. A village group must be small, and the leader must be under orders from the leader of the region. The activities of the group are concerned mainly with espionage, sabotage and propaganda. Members of the group have arms and explosives, but the objectives of their military opera- tions are determined by the commander of the guerrilla units in the region.

The group must help the guerrilla units in the region, give them information, and provide supplies. It is night work; and during the day members of the group must live like other villagers.

Towns

Guerrillas may infiltrate the outlying areas of towns and form special freedom fighter units. Their task is sabotage, propaganda and the acquiring and passing on of information. Attacks can be carried out at night on soli- tary members of the enemy forces and police. It is the re- sponsibility of members of town freedom fighter units to back up the revolutionary struggle by paralysing the economic life of the centre.

Discipline

There must be no abuse of power of any kind. A free- dom fighter who steals, loots, rapes or commits any other crime against the community must be tried and severely punished. It should be explained that such a breakdown in discipline endangers the whole revolutionary movement. Discipline comes from inner conviction. It is not a gift, but can be acquired by education, exercise and life in the guerrilla unit.

A suspected traitor should be tried by a military court and given every chance to defend himself. If found guilty, he must be shot.

Reconnaissance

This must be carried out ceaselessly so that the most up-to-date information is obtained about the enemy's position and strength. Information can be collected by :

    a. observation

b. the tapping of enemy telephone and radio messages

c. questioning local inhabitants

d. interrogating deserters and prisoners

e. reconnoitre in combat, i.e. the ambushing of an enemy unit and the seizing of equipment and prisoners

f. making use of the network of secret collaborators.

Information obtained from local inhabitants and from deserters and prisoners must always be verified, since the enemy uses agents to spread false information. Prisoners should be interrogated by the unit commander or an experienced member of the revolutionary, political organisation.

Interrogations should be conducted in secret and individually.

Prisoners

The question of prisoners, particularly during the initial stages of revolutionary warfare poses a number of problems.

A small unit of guerrillas, sometimes without even a base camp, cannot spare time, energy or supplies in looking after them. It is sometimes necessary to abandon them after seizing their weapons and supplies. In general, they should be treated as humanely as possible. If the enemy retains the hope that he can save his life by surrendering, his will to fight will be considerably reduced.

On the other hand, if the enemy is unaware of the moderate and humane treatment given by guerrillas to prisoners, he will fight with greater fury, in the belief that there is no escape.

When the revolutionary forces have liberated a considerable area, and have safe base camps, prisoners can be
taken, and made to do useful work.
Camouflage

The use of effective camouflage is of supreme importance, since the guerrilla's first duty is to remain hidden, and his camps, fortifications, arms depots etc. must be concealed
 both from land and from the air. Branches, grass, canes, straw and similar local materials should be used.

Each terrain has a dominant colour which must determine the colour of the guerrillas' clothing and equipment.

Acquisition of arms

At the start of guerrilla warfare, each unit acquires arms for its own use by :

   a. purchasing them

   b. raiding arms depots

   c. disarming enemy soldiers and police

   d. making them themselves

   e. obtaining them through workers in munitions factories.

For the acquisition of arms it is often sufficient to use rudimentary weapons such as knives, axes, assegais, sharpened canes, sabres etc. In this way the guerrilla unit arms itself little by little, and prepares the conditions for the acquisition of more arms.

Storage of arms

Arms should be stored in boxes lined with tin, and buried deeply in widely dispersed areas. The places where arms are stored should be known only to very few people, for example, unit and group leaders.

Arms and equipment should be regularly inspected and all metal parts protected against rust. A badly preserved weapon, or its loss, can cause the failure of an operation, and endanger the lives of every member of the unit.

Espionage

A spy serving the revolution is a comrade who pretends to be a friend of the enemy, and obtains and passes information of use in the waging of the revolutionary struggle.

Information should be sent via a third party, and if it is of crucial importance and urgent, by word of mouth.

The revolutionary double agent has a very important and difficult task. He must deceive the enemy and be unsuspected even by his closest friends. He must be in a position to obtain vital secret information about the enemy's strength and his plans, and know how to convey the information safely to the revolutionary forces. Where a counter-spy is a member of the enemy army he can give details

of the enemy's battle units, the disposition of troops, their morale, equipment and tactical and strategic plans. A very
important part of the help they can give is by leaving strategic points undefended in battle (e.g. with little ammunition
or in charge of a coward) so that these points can be easily captured. An officer in the enemy army who is a double agent, could be worth more than ten officers in the revolutionary forces.

Enemy spies and infiltrators

These must be tried by a military court, and if found guilty, sentenced to death. Each case must be thoroughly and carefully investigated before sentence is passed. Revolutionary intelligence agents may be mistaken for enemy spies and the danger of their condemnation must be guarded against.

Enemy attack

When fired on, comrades must immediately fall to the ground. Then, as soon as possible, each one should run in
a separate direction, look for a safe hiding place, and await calmly for the night.

In the darkness, contact can again be made through specially-arranged signals (animal and bird cries, drumming,
etc.) with the rest of the unit, and a new hiding place sought.

No attempt should be made to fight back. Only under very special conditions, when it is certain that casualties can be inflicted on the enemy, without the guerrillas suffering any loss, should a counter-attack be made. It must never be forgotten, that it is the task of the guerrilla not to fight or to provoke a fight, but to carry out the operation assigned to him, and then to disappear.

In general, the guerrilla shoots to demoralise the enemy and to keep him constantly on the alert. The enemy must
not be allowed to rest.

After an enemy attack, one or two comrades should stay behind to keep an eye on the enemy. If the enemy encamps,
the unit should be informed so that at night it may be fired on. Constant harassment of the enemy is the primary task of the guerrilla forces.

Sabotage

The enemy may be sabotaged in a number of ways, apart from the more obvious blowing up of bridges, railways, and key industrial points. For example:

i. Post Office employees can delay mail, "lose" official correspondence either by sending it to the wrong destination, or by preventing it from being delivered. They can scrutinise mail, and pass on important information to the guerrillas.

ii. Telephone company employees must listen in to all calls likely to be of interest in the revolutionary struggle, and see that any useful information is made known to the guerrillas.

iii. Garage attendants should adulterate petrol by adding sugar to it, put sand into the tanks of enemy army vehicles, and remove vital tools and spare parts.

iv. Drivers should cause accidents without arousing suspicion.

v. Teachers should tell their pupils that every one has a right to be free. They should explain the present African situation and the working of colonialism and neo-colonialism. Reference should be made to the liberated areas of Africa, and the progress being made there.

vi. Workers should stay away from work as often as they can, feigning illness. They should constantly seek ways of undermining the economic strength of the enemy.

vii. Civil servants should be as slack as possible in the carrying out of their duties. While pretending to be loyal to the oppressors they should continually criticize their policies to subordinates, and spread despondency and lack of confidence in the way the country is being administered. Tradesmen, engineers, etc., should block drains and pipes, cause electrical failures, etc., in the homes and offices of the enemy.

viii. Every member of the community can assist in the spreading of rumours, the creation of a general atmos- phere of discontent and unease, and in the under- mining of the enemy people's morale by making it apparent that they are unwelcome in the country and that they will shortly be ejected.

Attacking a village

Before an attack, as much information as possible should be obtained about the village and the local terrain. For ex- ample :
- a) Where the cables are (telegraphic and telephonic)
- b) How many people are armed
- c) If no-one is armed, how far away are the nearest armed men
- d) If there is a radio transmitter, or an amateur radio transmitter
- e) The names and whereabouts of traitors and colonial- ist agents.
- f) The location of bridges, roads, airfields, etc.

Once all this data has been collected, the appropriate files should be given to the operations section, and only after every detail has been examined should a decision be made whether or not to attack.

When an attack is decided upon the timing must be fixed, and the men chosen to carry out the attack, so that the operation may be carried out efficiently and successfully, each group acting independently from each other. One group will cut the telephone wires; a second, the telegraph cables; a third one will, with the help of villagers, search houses where there are arms and seize them. A fourth group will capture traitors and policemen. All these tasks should be carried out swiftly so that, apart from anything else, the guerrillas may impress the enemy with their efficiency, discipline and moral conviction. When the operation is concluded, the guerrilla forces must rapidly disappear from the village and hide once more in neighbouring territory.

Dead and wounded

If time allows, the dead should be buried. The wounded should, if possible, be carried to a safe place for treatment. Arms and equipment of dead and wounded must be retrieved immediately.

Defence of an occupied village

Each house should be regarded as a fortification to be connected with the next one by a trench about a metre deep. Revolutionaries should be able to pass safely from one house to another, protected from enemy fire. Barricades (made from bricks, stones, logs, furniture, etc.) should be prepared and ready to be put into position in streets where an enemy attack is imminent. In all houses, there should be holes made (just over the height of a man), through which the enemy may be fired on. To shoot, comrades should stand on a bench, box or stool in order to reach the necessary height. Enemy bullets entering through these holes when the guerrilla is moving around the room will be too high to do any damage. Villagers who are not prepared to assist in the fight should be compelled to leave the village.

Large villages where a considerable number of guerrillas are operating, should be divided up into zones, each zone being the responsibility of one leader. There should be one leader in supreme command.

If the enemy captures a house, smoke must be used, to halt the advance and provide cover by setting alight pre- pared old rags and other inflammable material soaked in petrol or oil.

In the course of the revolutionary armed struggle it will be necessary at times to destroy some of the country's assets, such as bridges, crops, buildings, airfields and telephone and telegraphic networks. Obviously no more de- struction will be carried out than is strictly necessary for the success of military operations.

Once colonialism and neo-colonialism have been totally defeated, and freedom attained, it will be comparatively easy, inspired by love of country, to rebuild what has been destroyed and for the people to advance to complete fulfilment.

Relations between revolutionaries and civilians

The guerrilla should always show gratitude for the food he eats in villages and homes. He should explain to the donor that the help he is giving to the guerrillas is assisting the progress of the revolutionary struggle which is liberating the people from colonialism and neo-colonialism.

Where possible, the guerrilla should help with house- work, farming and any other work needing to be done. At all times, the guerrilla must set an example of respect, hard work and devotion to the revolutionary cause.

Political work

Guerrilla forces are invincible because of their liaison with the masses. Propagandists must explain the revolu- tionary movement to the people, and see that they are informed of guerrilla victories. They should be people who have authority and influence in the region, particularly among the workers. Pamphlets, newspapers, broadcasts can all carry the message of the revolution. Discussion groups and meetings can be organised.

The more efficacious the propaganda work, the more rapidly will the public conscience be aroused. This in turn
will greatly affect revolutionary operations by ensuring mass support.

Those organising and carrying out guerrilla activities must be supplied with information of a political nature:

> i. the political composition of the area in which they are operating--political parties, aims, leadership, and the possibility of infiltration

ii. the reaction of the masses to the economic situation

iii. the degree of the people's collaboration with the enemy

iv. the morale of urban and agricultural workers

v. the response of the masses to revolutionary activities

vi. the centres of political life in the town or village

vii. the composition and strength of trade unions and such like organisations.

Civilian organisations

These play an important part in the liberation movement.

Their duties are manifold. They arrange the collection of contributions and taxes, maintain supplies, and spread propaganda. In enemy-held areas, civilian organisations must be clandestine.

In liberated areas it is necessary to establish administrative organs which should be responsible for the formulation of laws, rules and regulations for the administration of the zone. The establishment of political, economic and social instruments and their organisational techniques over the whole of the Continent must be built up on the basis of scientific socialism. The organs of the people's administration are vital factors in the liberation movement, and must be so organised as to become the nucleii from which the people's revolutionary states and the All-African Union Government will crystallise.

C. MATERIALS FOR DESTRUCTION

The manufacture and uses of destructive materials such as T.N.T., plastic bombs, dynamite, gunpowder, incen- diary bottles, detonators and lighting fuses, form part of the basic training of the freedom fighter. Recruits will be taught in the base training camps and workshops how to make them and the other many and varied weapons used by guerrilla units and by saboteurs operating within enemy-held positions.

The fully-trained guerrilla is armed both ideologically and physically for the revolutionary struggle. The tactics of guerrilla warfare rest in the main with him. With the support of the masses, and with unified direction of the revolutionary party, he is invincible.

People of Africa, arise!

Defeat imperialism, neo-colonialism and settler domination. Stand together and unite in the revolutionary struggle.

Forward to victory.

We shall conquer.